THE
REVOLUTION
IN
SALES
AND
MARKETING

THE REVOLUTION IN SALES AND MARKETING

Allan J. Magrath

amacom

AMERICAN MANAGEMENT ASSOCIATION

This publication is designed to provide accurate and authoritative information in regard to the subject matter covered. It is sold with the understanding that the publisher is not engaged in rendering legal, accounting, or other professional service. If legal advice or other expert assistance is required, the services of a competent professional person should be sought.

Library of Congress Cataloging-in-Publication Data

Magrath, Allan J.
    The revolution in sales and marketing / Allan J. Magrath.
        p. cm.
    Includes bibliographical references.
    ISBN 0-8144-5992-7
    1. Sales management. 2. Sales personnel—Effect of
technological innovations on. I. Title.
HF5438.4.M34   1990   90-304
658.8'1—dc20   CIP

Printing number

10 9 8 7 6 5 4 3 2 1

Joe and **Kerilee:**

As you go through life, may you never lose touch with what you believe in and care about most deeply. Be authentic and value your own distinctive talents.

Contents

Preface

The task of leadership is to make the status quo more dangerous than launching into the unknown.

—Sir John Harvey-Jones
Retired C.E.O., Imperial Chemical Industries
of the United Kingdom

Sales reps and managers are the infantry and platoon sergeants in the war for customers. And all around them the world is changing—transforming the nature of their jobs on the front lines and the survival skills required to reach their objective of profitable sales growth.

This is a book about coping with such change—about how sales reps and sales managers must develop new skills that will act as both a sword and shield in combatting competition.

The first half of the book outlines the biggest factors affecting sales reps. Chapter 1 examines how shifting customer targets by industry and city require changes in rep deployment. It also looks at changes in customer mind-sets and buying preferences, and implications of this for rep knowledge and sales proficiency.

Chapter 2 documents how competitor changes are altering the way reps are specialized and the emergence of new sales methods.

Chapter 3 details how distributors and resellers are shifting and what this means for sales reps who depend on such partnerships for sales success.

Chapter 4 provides an overview of how new technology tools can play a part in a rep's life—for better or worse.

So much for the foot soldiers. What about the sales managers who must manage the reps under new pressures? The last half of the book looks at the shape of things to come in sales force management.

Sales force management has traditionally centered around an eight-part task model. That is, sales managers do the following:

1. Find talented reps (or potential reps) by means of recruitment, screening, and selection.
2. Train reps.
3. Deploy reps in the field (e.g., by territory and account).
4. Supervise reps (e.g., with skills coaching, goal setting, and problem-solving leadership).
5. Measure rep results.
6. Evaluate rep performance in a two-way dialogue.
7. Reward reps (with incentives, compensation plans, and recognition programs).
8. Promote a select number of reps into management.

This model is decades old. Part II updates this model to bring it more in line with the new realities of selling and their effects on reps.

Chapter 5 examines how recruitment, selection, training, and deployment are different in an era of fluid sales teams or specialists; the need for lifelong rep learning; a more diverse rep mix including more women; college-educated reps; more varied distribution channels; and constantly shifting customer sets.

Chapter 6 discusses field leadership of reps and how it is so different today. New pressures are creating higher stress levels for both reps and managers. This chapter delineates how rep supervision is evolving during an era of wider spans of control and the somewhat less individual rep contact that results. Sales managers need to evolve from a "command and control" mentality to an "empower and coordinate" style of rep contact. In effect, managers assist reps in becoming "self-managed." The sales leadership task is to help this happen, with coaching that genuinely aids reps in working more intelligently. The chapter describes the four key ways managers coach and guide reps: by teaching them, mentoring them, helping them solve problems, and pathfinding for them.

Chapter 7 probes how traditional measurement and evaluation systems need to be updated to reflect new selling methods, such as solution selling and key account selling, and greater market volatility. The chapter discusses how to individualize pay plans to reward rep contributions to key priorities. Individualized pay plans become critical in a leaner postentrepreneurial workplace where reps need ample opportunity to grow their own pay checks by demonstrating both their skills and attainment of key management goals. The chapter deals at length with sales incentives and recognition and how to harness these for maximum rep motivation. The chapter also details a system for appraising reps that is high in rep involvement and geared to specific constructive actions that assist reps in improving their performance.

Chapter 8 describes how sales managers can manage the sales force for "total quality"—a concept more talked about than lived up to in the world of selling. In this connection, the components of a "total quality sales approach" are defined, including total quality in customer need fulfillment and quality in selling experiences. The chapter discusses the need to maximize customer "face-time" and wage a war on wasteful activities in the field that limit this contact.

Accounts are won or lost in field selling, which is the front line for both offense and defense in the fight for market share. The purpose of this book is to explore how externalities will play themselves out in shaping these front lines, with the hope that field reps and managers affected can better understand and respond to such changes with creativity and courage in their selling actions.

Acknowledgments

Although writing a book can be a solitary and often compulsive avocation, what results is ultimately the product of collaborative efforts. I'd like to acknowledge those who helped me along the way directly and indirectly. My typist, the cheerful and tireless Dianne Hall, and my editors at Amacom helped move the manuscript foreward and improved it. The ideas in the book are very much a result of my twenty years in sales and marketing—and all the fine executives and teachers who have taught or influenced me along the way: Cec Fitzwilliam, Bob Mayo, Charlie Broadwell, Jerry Maybrey, John Myser, Bud Johnston, Mike Leenders, Joe Kuhn, and Ken Hardy—men of great humor, insight, "street smarts," and character.

PART I

Environmental Turbulence and Sales Reps

Chapter 1

The Sales Revolution, Beginning With Customer Change

The years to come, however, will be unlike any we have seen before. The world will not stand still long enough to be studied. Times of turbulence are messy times. They require managers who have the courage to make decisions without complete information.

—Stephen C. Harper
Professor of management,
University of North Carolina
Quoted in *Business Horizons*, 1988

The Changing Customer Landscape

Sales reps exist to serve customers. So when customers change in major ways, reps must change as well. Customer change in the United States is occurring on four major dimensions.

1. Mature industries, and large accounts within them, are trimming their work forces and shedding ancillary businesses and products to focus on core markets.
2. New companies and new industries are emerging, growing from the seeds of market fragmentation, a

revitalized culture of entrepreneurship, a deregu-
lated economy, and newborn technologies.

3. City and state growth prospects are dramatically
   shifting because of the shifts in new industry creation
   and the declining fortunes of many industries hard
   hit by imported competition, such as the automobile,
   steel, machine tool, and textile industries.

4. On a less macro level, customer mind-sets are changing. There are rising demands for higher-quality
   products, more variety, and faster responsiveness. At
   the same time, many customers have less loyalty to
   specific vendors.

Each of these shifts holds promising opportunities for
sales reps who can adapt to them.

Restructuring and Downsizing

A time traveler from an earlier era who visited today's world
would be bewildered by its changes. The restructuring rate
among companies is growing faster than the sale of state
lottery tickets. Witness companies that no longer make or
sell what their names convey. B. F. Goodrich is a specialty
chemical company, not a producer of tires. Singer doesn't
make sewing machines, and Pullman doesn't build railcars.
B. F. Goodrich manufactures high-tech electronic systems,
while Singer is a holding company active in construction,
building, and industrial machinery markets. Greyhound
doesn't run a bus line, Lionel doesn't make electric trains,
and Chris Craft manufactures plastic bags, not cabin cruis-
ers.[1]

An industrial or commercial sales rep's favorite target is
often a Fortune 500-size company. Yet nowhere is there more
change than in these large companies. Between 1980 and
1988, the Fortune 500 eliminated 3.1 million jobs in the
United States.[2] In fact, during the 1983–1987 period, 1.5
million of this total job displacement occurred, although the
time frame was relatively prosperous for the American economy as a whole. Some large companies did grow in size and

scope, primarily through the addition of more geographic facilities. Examples include Federal Express, Wal-Mart Stores, Citicorp, and Holiday Inns. Only a select number of big companies grew their base businesses widely across all of their facilities, and these tended to be exemplary blue chip organizations such as IBM, 3M, McDonald's, American Express, or those engaged in basic fast-growth market niches such as Compaq Computer or Humana in high-tech or health care fields. In fact, four industries account for most of the top twenty-five fastest-growing large U.S. companies (see Figure 1-1).

Over 29 percent of Fortune 500 firms in 1970 no longer

Figure 1-1. The twenty-four U.S. companies that grew the fastest (from 1983 to 1987) among large companies and their respective industries.

Specialty Retailers	*Computers and Affiliated*
Businessland	Sun Microsystems
Price Co.	Compaq Computer
The Limited	Seagate Technology
Circuit City Stores	Cray Research
Nordstroms	Apple Computer
Toys R Us	Intergraph
Home Depot	Tandem Computers
Electronics and Telecommunications	*Wholesaling or Services/Other*
Emerson Radio	Liz Claiborne
Tele-Communications	Integrated Resources
Telex Corp.	Federal Express
MCI Communications	Reebok International
	M.D.C. Holdings
	Harvard Industries

Data originally contained in a more comprehensive article: Stuart Gannes, "America's Fastest-Growing Companies," *Fortune*, May 23, 1988, see especially chart on p. 31.

existed in 1981 because of mergers and leveraged buyouts. Merger activity in the 1980s more than doubled in numbers and increased more than five times in dollar volume. Leveraged buyouts in the United States increased from well under $15 billion in the early 1980s to over $100 billion by the end of the decade. In the appliance industry alone, the 1980s saw thirteen acquisitions or mergers take place, so that now only a handful of giants remain. In consumer products, five giant worldwide companies have emerged from a series of mergers (see Figure 1-2). These companies' combined sales exceeded the 1987 GNPs of Belgium, Denmark, Finland, Norway, Austria, and Switzerland. In some businesses, change was even more dramatic, occurring in less than half a decade. For instance, in textiles, between 1980 and 1985, 154,000 jobs were cut out as companies struggled to refocus and survive. The return on investment of U.S. textile mills fell from almost 12 percent in 1980 to 7.6 percent in 1985. Profits as a percentage of sales dropped by 50 percent. As a result, textile makers have become much more focused by selling off parts of their diversified companies to concentrate on businesses in which they can compete. J. P. Stevens bought Burlington's domestics division, while Burlington concen-

Figure 1-2. The world's top five consumer products companies.

	1987 Sales (billions of $)	Ownership
Philip Morris/General Foods/Kraft	$ 37.6	U.S.
Unilever	27.1	Dutch
Nestle	23.6	Swiss
Procter & Gamble	17.0	U.S.
RJR/Nabisco	15.9	U.S.
	$121.2	

Data originally contained in a more comprehensive article: *U.S.A. Today,* October 31, 1988, p. 1B.

trated more on carpets and bought C. H. Masland Carpet. West Point Pepperell sold its carpet division to Shaw, the big American carpet producer, and bought Cluett Peabody, a shirt manufacturer. In this way, West Point Pepperell can concentrate on its branded clothing lines such as Arrow Shirts and Burberry. The old economy of steel, chemicals, textiles, automobiles, appliances, tires, and heavy equipment continues to struggle and shake out. General Motors' market share is at an all-time low. USX (formerly U.S. Steel) has closed seven steel mills and cut its work force from 105,000 in the early part of the 1980s to 25,000 by late 1988. As one sage observer pointed out, "You are watching in manufacturing what has happened in agriculture—you need a much smaller work force to maintain your level of production."[3] To emphasize this point, one merely needs to look at a world-class resilient company such as Caterpillar Tractor. Under intense market competition from Japan's Komatsu, Caterpillar cut its work force from 79,000 to 53,000 and has hung on to compete effectively through automation and disciplined cost controls. This Caterpillar scenario is being played out in company after company, from John Deere to Ford.

A study of one industry, metalworking, showed that both average plant size and average employment is down, while the number of companies climbed 25 percent from 1972 to 1982.[4] The larger companies are becoming smaller entities by being less vertically integrated and by downsizing in focal parts of the business. This process has been termed *deglomeration.*

To a sales rep, such changes mean two things. First, new Fortune 500 companies must be targeted to replace previous prospects whose business performance is off. A rep has a tougher time selling to a struggling company unless his or her products have top-notch productivity benefits accruing from use. Second, where mergers have created an even larger entity or divestitures a smaller one, a rep must regauge the sales potential and reassess sales strategy and efforts. Sales managers in the midst of big company reorganizations and small company emergence may need to consider whether two different sales forces are needed to meet the needs of varied customers.

Growth Industries and New Industries

In the United States today, an entrepreneurial revolution is under way. Of the 14 million net new jobs created here from 1983 to 1987, most have come from what David Birch, an MIT economist, calls *the hidden economy*—the millions of privately held small companies rarely covered by the business press. Birch points out that since 1980 this country's hidden economy has created three times more jobs than Japan has. Each year, 600,000 new businesses start up, seven times the start-up rate in earlier postwar time frames. These new companies are creating new industries as they exploit technologies or cash in on the trend of the Fortune 500 giants to contract operations they formerly performed themselves to smaller companies.

In 1983, seven firms with aggregate sales of only $2 billion were just getting rolling in the computer business. These companies included Apple, Tandem, and Compaq Computer; as well as Cray Research, Intergraph, Seagate Technology, and Sun Microsystems. By 1988, only five short years later, their combined sales exceeded $7.7 billion.

Apple Computer alone employed 250 people in 1978, and 10,000 in 1988.

William Brock and David Evans, two economists, in their influential book *The Economics of Small Business* (New York: Holmes & Meier, 1986), point out that the change to an entrepreneurial economy is a historic shift—reversing the previous century's trend toward bigness in both American companies and their percentage of total U.S. economic activity.

The average size of all U.S. companies increased up until the mid-1970s and then turned around. Company sizes shrank, self-employment rose, and small companies' share of the GNP increased. This was true of not only service businesses but manufacturing companies as well.

Entrepreneurs have stepped forward to start up all kinds

of strange and wonderful businesses. Second Wind of Paso Robles, California, sells bottled cleaner to keep sneakers from getting dirty. It was started by a 28 year old who used his college trust fund as seed money. Sanford Ziff is a 63-year-old optometrist who started a chain of high-fashion sunglass shops that now operate in 200 shopping malls in the United States (Sunglass Huts of America). Donald Beaver, Jr., manufactures oil-absorbing products used to clean up grime from factory floors. His sales have gone from nothing in 1985 to over $10 million in 1989, and his company employs 139 people. Gerald Goldhaber researches what should be on product warning labels and consults on the results. He keeps fifty people employed and grossed $2 million in 1987. *Forbes* magazine describes all this entrepreneurship as producing "a more complex, more specialized and more efficient economy."[5]

Many medium-size, niche-based companies have rivaled the financial results of larger counterparts in their industries. Figure 1-3 showcases some of these outstanding performers. New industries are emerging as well. In the 1970s, biotechnology was an infant, uncertain industry. In the late 1980s, new products from this technology are being produced to treat diabetes, hemophilia, growth problems in children, and even milk production in cattle. And biotechnology exploitation has given both renewed growth to old companies such as Monsanto and a whole new start to companies such as Genentech. In the short span of fifteen years, an industry has moved from the world of ideas to full-blown commercialization.

Over 25 million people in the United States now manage commercial businesses from their homes on either a full- or part-time basis. New distribution channels such as warehouse clubs are springing up to service such entrepreneurs.

The implications for sales organizations of the entrepreneurial growth of new companies and new industries is that entirely new accounts must be identified, and often new distribution set up to cover them. Where these organizations are very small, average sales per order for a company selling to them may also be small. This may require creative lower-cost approaches such as teleselling or direct marketing via

Figure 1-3. Small- to medium-size companies with outstanding financial results.

	Five-Year Return on Equity	1987 Sales (in millions)	1987 Profits (in millions)	Other Giants in Its Industry
1. Tootsie Roll Industries (candy)	19.3%	$115	$15.7	Mars
2. A. T. Cross (pens)	21.6	206	31.4	BIC, Parker, Papermate
3. Neutrogena (cosmetics)	34.6	168	21	Estee Lauder, Maybelline, Revlon
4. New England Business Services (office forms)	24.1	217	22	Crain, Moore Corp.
5. Diagnostic Products (medical diagnostic kits)	18.5	41	11	Johnson & Johnson, Abbot Labs
6. Pratt and Lambert (paints, specialty coatings	17.4	231	9	Pittsburg, Sherwin Williams

Data originally contained in a more comprehensive article: "Best Small Companies in America," *Forbes*, November 14, 1988, pp. 285–304.

mail-order catalog. To prospect for business, new data bases must be purchased by marketing departments and screened for potential. Sales lead-generating programs become more necessary than ever because turnover among new businesses and entrepreneurs is high, and sales force productivity will suffer unless careful targeting gets priority.

Shifting Geographic Potentials

Quite apart from the fact that sales organizations must rejuggle call priorities based on the shifting attractiveness of their large, medium, and small account mix, another change is occurring. Major dislocations in the geographic account potentials of different American cities and states is occurring. Economic change has punished or rewarded various regions differentially, based on their industry dependencies, their success in attracting new industries, and their resource availability to support business (e.g., clean water and transportation systems).

Cities where industrial growth is down include Detroit; Houston, Texas; Denver; and New Orleans, who strongly depend on depressed markets such as oil, mining, or U.S.-made autos. Cities enjoying a boom include Boston; Austin, Texas; Atlanta; and San Francisco, where new industries or growth industries such as software, electronics, biotechnology, fiber optics, or broadcasting are doing well.

In parts of the Rust Belt, entrepreneurs have created new high-tech companies in what *Fortune Magazine* calls "the ruins of yesterday's industry." Pittsburgh is an example of this phenomenon. Over 650 new-growth companies in the Pittsburgh area employ 77,000 people. In 1978, the "Steel City" employed 222,000 in manufacturing and 72,000 in primary metal production. By 1982, 46,000 manufacturing jobs were gone and 23,000 primary metal jobs were cut back. By 1988, primary metal job employment was at 26,000, down by two thirds. However, other new businesses picked up the slack, including health and financial services, food processing, machinery, glass and scientific instrument manufacturing, and retailing, so that today only 13 percent of Pittsburgh's work force of 975,000 are involved in manufacturing jobs. Pittsburgh has clearly made a comeback.

Unemployment, which in Michigan hit 17 percent in 1982 has also decreased because of new businesses such as robotics manufacturing and turnarounds engineered within core industries such as machine tools.

In other U.S. cities, revived growth has come from both diversification of jobs and favorable entrepreneurial efforts.

Charlotte, North Carolina, jumped from the sixty-sixth fastest-growing U.S. city to thirty-second as a result of banking deregulation and because new banks chose Charlotte as a home base for operations. Seattle, Washington, once very dependent on aerospace, moved from sixty-fifth among growth-ranked cities to fortieth because of the success of new businesses such as freight forwarders.

Many small towns in the United States have also seen dramatic growth shifts. For instance, Japanese auto plants have located in Flat Rock, Michigan (Mazda), Lafayette, Indiana (Subaru-Isuku), Marysville, Ohio (Honda), Georgetown, Kentucky (Toyota), and Smyrna, Tennessee (Nissan). The plants have brought boom times to these little towns by adding thousands of direct and indirect jobs to nearby feeder plants or services.

To a sales force covering states or cities, such dramatic shifts make obsolete many territory boundaries that were drawn to equalize sales potential. Such boundaries now need to be redrawn to accommodate the shifting fortunes of the area accounts.

Shakeouts and Start-Ups: New Customer Priorities

Aside from shifting account prospects and geographic territory realignments, sales reps are also affected by changes in the mind-sets of customers. As these economic waves have radically washed across the nation, changes in customer thinking are altering the world of selling—whether sales reps work for manufacturers and service providers or for retailers and wholesalers.

Smarter Customers

The customer has become more sophisticated. The *world*, not merely North America, is now the shopping mall for customers. A consumer doesn't just buy Kodak film for her camera, but also Fuji. The choice of a car is broader than it has ever been, with more Japanese than American car producers manufacturing in North America. In 1987 and 1988, the top companies registering patents in the United States were both Japanese—Canon KK and Hitachi Ltd. The giants in electronics and communications in America such as RCA, Motorola, and General Electric, must now share center stage with Japan's Matsushita, Toshiba, NEC, or Germany's Sieman's and Korea's Samsung. It is Imperial Chemicals Inc. of Britain that owns Sherwin Williams Paint Co., not an American organization. Sales reps face smarter customers who often buy from global companies when they are looking for products. This applies to purchasing agents in industry as well as to householders looking for a VCR, a microwave, or a wristwatch. Just to illustrate that no market is immune from global competitors, Okamoto Industries of Japan announced plans to seek 5 to 10 percent of the U.S. condom market, using a multi-million-dollar ad campaign stressing product quality. This company has 60 percent of Japan's market for condoms. As a result of global competition, sales reps must know a wider array of worldwide competitors and be able to sell against more offerings. This calls for greater professionalism in sales technique and an appreciation of the selling strengths and weaknesses of foreign companies a rep may have never sold against.

Customers' Demand for Quality

Today's customers are quality conscious. Any company with third-rate offerings will not even get through the door. When Jaguar's product quality deteriorated in the 1970s, its sales plummeted. When Xerox didn't produce the best small copiers in the world, it got knocked off its perch by the Canons, Sharps, and Minoltas of Japan. In industry, customers concerned about quality will often source (buy) 100 percent of their orders from a single vendor who can meet their demanding specifications. The magazine *Economist* has forecast that by 1995 the trend among automakers to single source auto components will lead to only fifty large specialized vendors manufacturing only a limited line of components (such as Eaton in transmissions and Bosch in lighting).

Sales reps who sell to such demanding single-sourcing customers must learn how to sell to their upper managements, who usually have the last word on these critical decisions. Reps must be as comfortable dealing with senior management in a customer's decision-making echelon as selling to user departments. For example, General Motors Saturn Division plant has gone to single sourcing of a variety of products, as has General Electric, whose appliance division awarded a $70 million single-source contract to Cameron & Barkley Co. of Charleston, South Carolina. This move cut out purchases from 2,000 suppliers of maintenance, repair, and operating supplies and was made at the most senior level within General Electric.

Consumers in retail markets are also hooked on quality. The Japanese car makers, having attracted loyal customers to their small and mid-sized cars, are now moving these buyers up-market to their luxury nameplates (such as Honda's Acura). Consumers are flocking to buy from retailers who can provide them with the total-quality merchandise they want. Witness the success of The Limited and Nordstroms in clothing, L.L. Bean in the catalog business, and Carson Pirie Scott in department stores.

Sales reps and managers must be much more professional in all respects to convey total quality, then gain and hold on to loyal customers.

Once all companies' product offerings become equally excellent, one of the best ways to differentiate one company from another is by its sales force. The value-added to customers becomes the way the product is sold, not just the product itself. *Sales and Marketing Management* magazine annually conducts surveys to determine the best American sales forces by industry. The Sales Force Award winners, whether they are involved in industrial, commercial, health care, service, or retail markets, all differentiate themselves from competitors in a half-dozen ways. Companies such as Caterpillar Tractor save their construction contractors money by helping them get a better return on their investment in equipment. Companies such as Black and Decker help retail customers boost their returns on inventory investment with excellent co-op ad plans and merchandising supports, presented by their sales force.

Du Pont provides value-added by having its reps and technical personnel customize products to meet exact customer needs. Financial services giants such as Merrill Lynch or Northwestern Mutual Life Insurance outshine rivals by fielding the best-trained sales reps or agents in the business. This inspires confidence in customers looking for financial investments and security. Corning Glass Works and Scott Paper have reps who assist retailers to optimize display space, with suggested display configurations to fit their type of store and regional product-assortment preferences.

For each of these companies, valued-added is as evident in a quality sales force as it is in quality products and services.

Customers' Demand for Rapid Response

Today's customer is busier, opting for companies that can cater to scarcity and offer responsive service. Consumers are buying by mail, television, and catalog in increasing numbers as their shopping time becomes more and more limited by careers and leisure-time pursuits. Industry customers have a new-found sense of urgency for a different reason. Life cycles of product options and features are shorter, and many industrial companies are managing time for competitive advantage by incorporating new product or system advantages as quickly as possible. In Japan, Toyota has compressed the total time it takes to sell, order, build, and deliver a new car to a Japanese family to eight days (including two days to assemble the car to the customer's spec). This time responsiveness used to be twenty-six days, or three times longer! The sales representative at a Toyota dealership therefore has a distinct advantage over others at competing auto companies such as Nissan, Honda, or Mazda. Responsiveness to customers is becoming even more important in businesses such as insurance. AAL, a fraternal society that operates a large insurance business in the United States, recently reorganized the entire company of five hundred clerks, technicians, and managers, in order to cut the cumbersome time to process insurance cases from over twenty days to five days or less.[6]

Sales representatives at companies pushing to become more time responsive must learn to decrease the time needed to launch new products into national distribution. Often this means skipping regional sales rollouts and going full speed into the total countrywide product launch without the benefit of "starting small" in an area and learning slowly how to position the item. In the case of direct selling, the rep must learn to penetrate a market with less motion wasted to find the product's best prospective users. In addition, with time urgency a new concern of customers, companies must flatten their sales organizations to minimize ponderous decision making.

Customers' Demand for Variety

Today's customers are also demanding more variety in product and service offerings, and they are getting it. A traveler can choose from budget rental cars, no-frill motels, and economy airline flights, can go for luxury on all three of these services, or can get any variation in between these extremes. A small-business customer choosing a personal computer, printer, software, and modem has so many choices of makes and models, with varied prices and features, that entire consultant practices exist simply to help sort through the labyrinth of options.

The existence of so many choices has two big impacts on sales representatives in consumer or industrial markets. First, since customers are often confused by so much choice, they want and need to buy *solutions*, not just products. Solutions selling is aggressively practiced by Bell Atlantic in Philadelphia. Its account executives solve the operating problems of Bell's three operating companies by selling a variety of technologies—from office automation products to computer networking solutions, from technical solutions to data transmission issues. Steelcase no longer sells just desks or filing cabinets; it now sells total office systems, from layout design to color-coordinated furniture, partitions, shelving, office computers, and accessories.

Solutions selling has a broader meaning than just meeting all of an industry's or account's needs. When companies such as Clark (maker of industrial forklifts) and Caterpillar (construction equipment) sell solutions via their reps, they justify their equipment prices over the total life-cycle cost equation. They recognize that the customer is not merely buying a lift truck's initial price, but all the costs that accompany the truck's use, including fuel, maintenance, operator, and salvage costs. The rep justifies pricing in terms of the whole "solution" being purchased by the customer. The customer, concerned about total machine costs, not merely the initial price, wants a solution price that holds total costs in check. It does no good, for example, to save money on the initial cost of a forklift, only to pay later with higher maintenance costs and downtime operator salary costs. Sales reps who deliver solutions will prosper whether the sale is a home video entertainment center from Sears or a computer-integrated manufacturing network from Digital Equipment.

Second, in an era of multiple customer choices, sales reps must learn new teamwork skills, since the knowledge they individually possess about specific products is insufficient in many instances to satisfy the customized solutions consumers demand. The rep is a member of a team that includes product specialists in marketing, customer service personnel handling order logistics, and technical personnel with diagnostic, repair, installation, and user-training skills. It is often the team that consummates the sale, not the individual sales rep. A car dealership with a great team of sales personnel, a fine service crew, and an excellent financial specialist will often win out over a dealership where sales people make promises without consulting the rest of the team.

In an industrial setting, can you imagine a company selling a CAD-CAM system of workstations to an engineering firm, without the teamwork of hardware specialists, software/programming experts, and technical repairmen? Teamwork and coordination is one of today's key prerequisites for a successful sales organization. But more than interfunctional team cooperation is needed. In complex multinational accounts with multiple buying locations, "team selling" is vital between sales reps in the same company. This is because customers become very aware of discrepancies in prices, terms, delivery, and other factors between their various locations serviced by a common vendor. The sales rep as lone-wolf performer is a declining reality in many industries. Figure 1-4 illustrates this notion of a customer-handling team. Sony, when launching its Pro Mavica professional still video camera, used a multifunction team, including engineers, sales specialists handling national accounts, and marketing personnel. The team worked together to improve the earliest prototype models to fit customer needs more exactly. In addition, the team decided how to position the product in advertising and which customer segments to target first, and it monitored customer satisfaction after the product was out in the market.

Du Pont's Electronics division uses a team selling approach to handle key electronics companies in locations such as California's Silicon Valley or Route 128 in Boston. An account executive is a central point of contact for Du Pont's sales efforts, and this person coordinates a team of multiple talents including design engineers, technical service specialists, and others. Du Pont's purpose is not just to provide close customer communication and comprehensive account coverage: But because original equipment manufacturers (OEMs) in electronics do more single sourcing, this kind of intensive account servicing is vital for competitive survival.[7]

From Technical Selling to "Service" Selling:
The Story of Linde Gas

To illustrate how selling orientations must change to accommodate new customer changes, consider the case of Linde, Union Carbide's Toronto-based subsidiary selling industrial, medical, and specialty gases. For many years, its sales focus was to emphasize the technical superiority of its products

Figure 1-4. The customer-handling team.

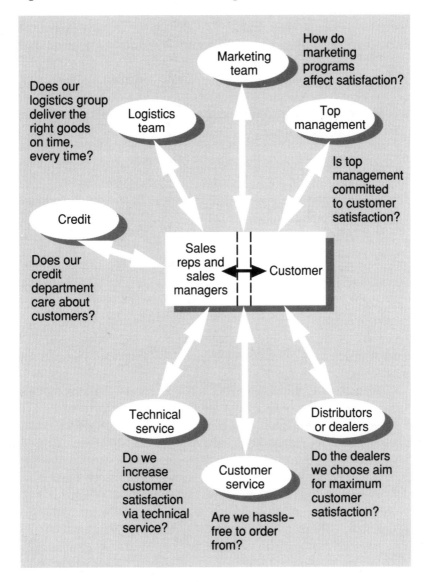

and its superior engineering consultants who back up the sales force. Linde decided to conduct research with its customers to see if they wanted to buy what it was selling. In focus groups, customers told them that Linde's and its competitors' products and technical backup were equal. The focus groups revealed, however, that customers were concerned more with "service" than products or even technical advice per se. And service, in separate research (from a wider two hundred-customer sample), was defined by Linde as providing:

- Problem-solving skills in the use of its gases
- Flexibility in meeting customers' specific individualized application needs
- Complaint-handling promptness and cooperation with respect to gases

Linde also recognized that these key valued services were not solely the responsibility of the sales force. The whole seven hundred-person customer-handling and contact team, from truck drivers and dispatchers to technical consultants and managers, could affect aspects of these service dimensions.

As a result, the company has reoriented its sales force to emphasize service and provided reps with many sales aids valued by customers, such as "customer friendly" wall charts and brochures about the safe handling and storage of its gases. In addition, it emphasized the importance of teamwork and cooperation in caring about customers by putting all seven hundred customer contact personnel (including the sales force) through an intensive two-day training workshop reorienting them to what customers really want in service. The workshop emphasized how Linde must consistently display its customer helpfulness across all jobs in the company. Internal cooperation was highlighted as an area where Linde must improve; if sales personnel promised service and were then unable to deliver it because of internal communication problems, the whole service strategy would be at risk.

The response by customers to Linde's changes has been overwhelmingly positive. As a result, Linde has carried its customer service message into all its advertising media *and* has trained its distributors with the two-day workshop process.

This example illustrates how selling organizations must work as an integral team with all other customer contact departments. And it highlights how reps must sell much more than products or even an augmented notion of products, including technical advice. They must sell what the customers care about—from rapid responsive complaint handling to quality assurance in products, continuity of problem-solving skills, and many other aspects of service, over and above the price performance of the products themselves.

Customers' Demand for No-Hassle Guarantees

Customers are so fed up with poor after-sales service or inattention to their needs that they will beat a path to the door of any company that performs "as advertised" unconditionally. Lincoln Electric Co., the Cleveland-based maker of arc welding equipment, guarantees its customers will save a predetermined amount of money on their purchases. Its salespeople present detailed savings proposals to customers; if such savings do not completely materialize, Lincoln pays the customer the difference.

If you return boots bought from L. L. Bean ten years after they've been purchased, you get a sales credit, a refund, or replacement boots, no questions asked. L. L. Bean is thriving.

"Bugs" Burger bug killers promise bug "extermination," not "pest control." If they don't satisfy customers 100 percent, customers do not have to pay a cent. "Bugs" Burger has the highest market share in this very fragmented business and yet charges ten times (in some cases) what its competitors charge.[8]

If Boeing receives an order for an aircraft part for a plane that is on the ground and out of service, it provides the part in two hours, even if it must strip the part from an airplane on its own assembly line.

When John Deere got into the four-wheel drive tractor market, its products had reliability problems. It promised each farmer who bought the tractors that these problems would be remedied as quickly as possible, at no cost whatsoever to him. It kept every one of these promises.[9] As a result, its market share is very high in this business.

Sales representatives must become customer advocates in a world where the customer demands fair, honest, and guaranteed service. The sales organization must take the initiative to do what is right and is in their customers' best interests. In addition to this more important "advocacy" role, the sales organization more than ever before must know the customer's industry and have a wide array of multiple contacts in the customer's business. The rep must often become a vertical industry specialist, immersing him or herself in the client's business and industry. Kodak's high-speed copier sales reps know as much about the problems and challenges of running "quick copy print shops" as do the owners of these businesses. A sales rep at Ethan Allen Furniture is a decorating consultant who can converse knowledgeably about almost any aspect of house decor.

Ballard Medical's Sales Team

Consider the case of Ballard Medical Products. This $10 million specialty manufacturer of products for intensive care units in hospitals exists despite giant rivals such as Baxter-Travenol and Johnson & Johnson. The reason? Ballard's sales force immerses itself with both the decision makers who order and specify their products and the real users of the products.[10]

Ballard people work and hold key meetings with all the multiple influencers in accounts, from critical care directors to directors of respiratory therapy and infection control, and head nurses. These reps often spend eighteen-hour days at hospitals, working with nurses who use Ballard trachea suction devices on patients hooked up to respirators. Ballard's personnel are truly application specialists, while their diversified rivals' sales forces are spread across multiple product lines. Ballard knows its user customers by name and regularly launches new products that originated from this high customer intimacy. For example, it came up with Ready Care, a kit consisting of gloves, a mask, and an eye shield to protect hospital workers treating AIDS patients, as a result of nursing suggestions it received while working on wards, detailing other products.

Customer mind-set shifts are having a marked and lasting impact on sales organizations. Figure 1-5 summarizes these macrochanges.

Summary

Customer shifts are pushing reps to ascend to new levels of expertise that can be defined in total as a commitment to a *higher order of sales professionalism*. This professionalism manifests itself in their depth of industry acumen, their pursuit of customer needs, their solutions-selling orientation, and their teamwork with other key members of the "total customer contact team." This higher order of professionalism often results in the reps managing their territories as *businesses*, with themselves at the center of the business, as territory managers. One company, PPG Industries, has gone so far as to provide its sales rep "territory managers" with a territory income statement, issued quarterly so the reps are aware of how their territory results fit into the company's overall profitability.

The upshot of customer changes is that reps are evolving as more confident individuals and team players. They are having to develop customer partnerships and stronger relationships in an era when such customers are unrelenting in their demands for responsive service, total need solutions, zero-defect quality, and limitless product variety. Unless a company's top reps can evolve toward this synergy with customers, the company will lose market share.

The shifting prospects of companies, determined by industry city and state, are forcing reps to resize sales potentials, retarget sales efforts to different companies, and

Figure 1-5. Macrochanges in sales organizations.

Major Customer Shifts in Mind-Set	Impact on Sales Reps
Smarter customers—with global-brand consciousness and single-sourcing desires	Reps must know and be able to sell against more competitors with "provable" benefits. They must be as comfortable selling to upper management as to the product users and purchasing personnel.
Quality-conscious customers	Heightened need for sales reps to project total professionalism to secure customer loyalty. Reps become the value-added, as much as products.
Customer desire for rapid responses to their needs	Sales reps must learn faster and focus on prime customer prospects for their products, in much less time.
Customer desire for variety, but frequent confusion over proliferating product choices	Sales reps must sell total solutions and must work as part of a *team* of "customer handlers" to provide the credibility and assurances customers need.
Customer expectation of unconditional, service guaranteed	Sales reps must act as customer advocates to be certain their companies *deliver* on promises made to customers. In addition, sales forces must anticipate customer needs proactively by becoming industry and client specialists in selected important end-user markets.

sort out how to sell to smaller or medium-size companies efficiently.

In short, reps are having to alter the way they sell, to whom they sell, and where they sell—changes so dramatic it is not an overstatement to suggest that a sales revolution is in progress across the United States.

Further Readings

Band, Bill. "The Real Sale Begins After the Sale." *Sales and Marketing Management Canada* (September 1988), pp. 27–29.

Bertrand, Kate. "Sony: Sorting Out the Sales Suspects." *Business Marketing* (August 1988), pp. 44–46. A detailed write-up on how a customer-handling team operates.

Birch, David L. "The New Economy—What Goes Up . . ." *Inc.* Magazine (July 1988), pp. 25–26. Also see his column "After the Crash" in *Inc.* Magazine (December 1988), pps. 29–30.

Byrne, John. "Is Your Company Too Big?" *Business Week* (March 27, 1989), pp. 84–94. Profiles how small companies are fueling U.S. job creation and industry innovation.

Case, John. "The Disciples of David Birch." *Inc.* Magazine (January 1989), pp. 39–45.

Drucker, Peter F. *Innovation and Entrepreneurship.* New York: Harper & Row, 1985, esp. pp. 1–17 on "the Entrepreneurial Economy."

Gannes, Stuart. "America's Fastest Growing Companies." *Fortune*, May 23, 1988, pp. 28–40.

Hanan, Mack. *Consultative Selling*, 3rd ed., New York: AMACOM, 1985.

"JIT Seen as a Growing Trend." *Industrial Distribution* (August 1988), pp. 9–10. A report on Touche Ross & Company's Survey of Just-in-Time Implementation by American Business.

Kotkin, Joel, and Sara Baer-Sinnott. "Hot Spots, Metropolitan City Growth Rankings." *Inc.* Magazine (March 1989), pp. 90–92.

Leavitt, Theodore. "The Pluralization of Consumption." *Harvard Business Review* (July–August 1988), pp. 7–8.

Machan, Dyan. "How Gus Blythe Smelled Opportunity." *Forbes*, October 3, 1988, pp. 104–113. Chronicles all manner of new start-ups.

Olsen, Richard J. "Niche Shock and How to Survive It," *Planning Review* (July–August 1988), pp. 6–13.

Peters, Tom. "The Destruction of Hierarchy." *Industry Week* (August 15, 1988), pp. 33–35.

———. "Creating the Fleet Footed Organization," *Industry Week* (April 18, 1988), pp. 35–39.

Starry, Claire, and Nick McGaughey. "Growth Industries: Here Today, Gone Tomorrow." *Business Horizons* (July–August 1988), pp. 69–74.

Zakon, Dr. Alan, and Richard W. Winger (of the Boston Consulting Group). "Consumer Draw—From Mass Markets to Variety." *Management Review* (April 1987), pp. 20–27.

Zeithaml, Valarie A. "Consumer Perceptions of Price, Quality and Value: A Means-End Model and Synthesis of Evidence." *Journal of Marketing* (July 1988), pp. 2–22.

———. "Quality as a Competitive Strategy. *Marketing Science Institute Report* No. 87-114 (December 1987), pp. 20–23; and with Czepiel, John. "The Concepts of Customer Loyalty and Customer Relationships." *Marketing Science Institute Report* No. 87-114 (December 1987), pp. 24–25.

Chapter 2

Tougher Competition, New Sales Methods

Every day some young business person in Singapore or India, in Brazil or Italy or Germany is writing a business plan in which he is determined to export one third and probably half his product to the U.S. marketplace.

—Ohio Governor Richard Celeste
September 15, 1988

The Changing Competitor Lineup

Just as customers have changed, so too have competitors. And competitor shifts have altered the selling game as much as changing customers have. Where new customer priorities require a higher order of sales professionalism today, competitor shifts mandate higher productivity from any sales force.

American consumers in 1988 have over 500 models of videocassette recorders to choose from.

In 1986 there were *twelve* IBM personal computer clones. In 1987, a year later, there were *two hundred* such competitors.

Markets are becoming ever more crowded, and with such crowding and marketplace saturation, prices are under extreme stress. So too are the margins of those who manufacture these products.

So intense is the advent of new global competitors that,

27

according to *The Wall Street Journal*,[1] even the Japanese are crying out for tariff protection as their home market is being flooded with cheap imports from South Korea and Taiwan. Japan's large department stores Jusco and Daiei are beginning to sell all sorts of electronic products from newly industrialized nations, just as K-Mart and Sears did with Japanese products during earlier decades in the United States.

Once a market becomes "hot," it attracts multiple voracious competitors in almost no time at all. *U.S.A. Today* reports that the market for large-size women's clothing is growing 33 percent per year compared to the total market growth of only 7 percent.[2] The result? The number of apparel manufacturers making size 14 clothes and larger for women grew from 250 in 1983 to 1,200 in 1988.

The Emergence of Nontraditional Forms of Competition

In certain markets, not only are competitors more numerous, they are often different. For instance, in the automotive industry joint ventures between car companies have created myriad hybrid competitors. Mazda is now 25 percent-owned by Ford, so its plant in Flat Rock, Michigan, produces the Ford Probe model car. Ford has also entered into an agreement with Nissan to build a front-wheel-drive minivan outside Cleveland in a joint venture plant.[3] General Motors already has joint venture factories with Suzuki in Canada (Cami plant in Ingersoll, Ontario) and with Toyota in California (Summi plant). Chrysler has agreements with Mitsubishi motors and only recently acquired American Motors' Jeep and Renault's Premier lines of cars. It is getting so that it is difficult to know who is a competitor in some markets without a program.

The Impact of Tougher Competition on Sales Organizations

Sales organizations are being dramatically affected by competitors in two crucial ways. Because so many more competitors are chasing after the same number of customers (due to slow-growth economies), sales organizations are putting great emphasis on *retaining* customers. At companies such as Metropolitan Life Insurance Co., this focus on retaining customers has resulted in two major sales thrusts—sales reps must speak to customers in language they understand, not "insurance jargon," and every sales rep is personally responsible for his customers. If a customer has a problem, a rep must follow through to fix it and cannot pass the customer off to another department.

In the course of retaining accounts, many sales organizations are using new ways to service customers, such as Teleselling for small accounts, and are appointing national account managers for large, vitally important multisite accounts. The push for productivity is generating these new selling platforms.

Second, some companies are bundling together all the products they market and targeting specific industries. They are then setting up market-centered specialized sales organizations to cater to these specific industries. Hewlett Packard has a separate sales organization for aerospace customers, while General Electric has such a group of sales specialists and engineers targeted toward the power generation market. 3M has automotive centers in Detroit, Michigan, in Germany, and in Japan to serve domestic and foreign makers. IBM has a specialized market-centered sales group for hospital customers. Xerox has an operating unit to sell complex systems to the U.S. federal government and large corporate clients. This Xerox organization is so oriented to customers that it is allowed to sell both Xerox and non-Xerox products to meet the clients' needs. By targeting specific markets with new organizational sales units, these companies can often develop specialized custom products for these distinct-end customers.

Sony, for example, recently organized a sixteen-person sales, marketing, and technical task force to focus on sales of professional still video cameras to Fortune 500 companies, real estate companies (to photograph property), law enforcement agencies (for crime documentation), and publishers (for electronic news gathering).[4] This task force, because it concentrated on discovering the different needs of each specialized segment, came up with different product design ideas for the different users. Some users such as publishers wanted very lightweight equipment for news gathering, while others such as real estate brokers wanted "point and shoot" camera-operating simplicity.

New Organizations With New Tasks

As selling margins have been squeezed by more numerous competitors and the need to retain customers has gained urgency, sales organizations have moved from generalist, territorially based organization to more levels of speciality. The old lone-wolf sales model of one sales rep managing all the business in a territory is being updated and supplemented with specialists in telephone selling, vertical industry, and national accounts. Each of these new systems operates differently than would a horizontal "full product bag" sales force, selling to all prospective accounts in a region. For instance, Scott Paper's consumer division, once organized by sales rep territory, today rewards sales reps by accounts serviced. In this way, a Scott Paper rep's compensation is tied to the fortunes of the customers he/she services instead of a region's results, which do not reflect a customer's total disparate locations.

Telesales Organizations

Teleselling is becoming an increasing reality in a great many companies. Sales organizations are having to jump into telesales with both feet for two reasons. First, depressed prices as a result of more competition are pinching gross margins. In addition, selling costs for regular face-to-face sales calls continue unabated. McGraw-Hill, in its biennial cost-of-sales-call data, shows sales cost increases are not occurring (or even price *decreases* are the rule).

Figure 2-1 shows the average cost of a face-to-face sales call from 1977 to 1987. Although these numbers are slightly

Figure 2-1. The average cost of a face-to-face sales call in the United States.

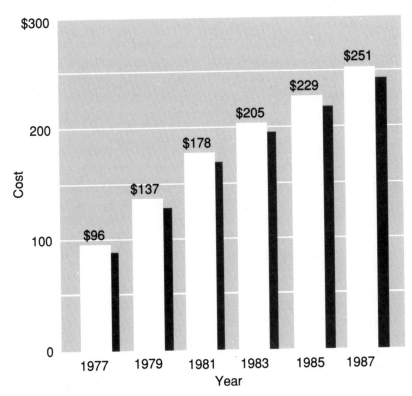

Data originally contained in a more comprehensive article: "Growth Rate Slows for Average Sales Call Cost," *Business Marketing* , July 1988, p. 16.

lower for companies relying more on dealers and distributors, the upward trend line is still apparent over time, though it has slowed somewhat since 1985. In Western Europe, sales call costs are even higher at $640 per call, due to both higher airline fares and steeper hotel rates (compared with those in the United States).[5]

The cost of selling isn't the only issue in productivity. Studies by McGraw-Hill laboratory consistently show that of total time available for reps to sell, only about 40 percent is used in face-to-face calls. The balance is spent traveling, at meetings, doing paperwork, or handling complaints.

The Conference Board study of telesales (Report No. 912, "A Growing Role for Business to Business Telemarketing," by Earl Bailey, 1988) found that one in four of the broad sample of 214 companies are teleselling, and even more than that expect to use teleselling in the future.[6] Some companies use teleselling as their only means of sales, while others are using it to supplement the regular field sales force.

The Conference Board reports that most companies start small with telesales efforts, merely trying to relieve the load on field sales reps or to provide a 1-800 phone number to handle customer inquiries. Experience is often so excellent with proactive teleselling that activities of telesales personnel are subsequently enlarged and managed as separate organizational entities.

Strategic Issues in Teleselling

There is little doubt that companies find the telephone efficient. After all, a skilled telesales person can make anywhere from twenty to forty calls per day. Face-to-face rep calls average anywhere from four to eight per day. Responding to customer phone inquiries is less time-consuming than answering them by mail. Over a thousand leads can be qualified by a trained telesales rep in twenty working days. Costs per call in teleselling range around $8 to $10, according to companies such as Skyway Freight Systems of Santa Cruz, California, which uses teleselling extensively.[7]

The strategic issues involved in making teleselling pay off appear to be threefold: (1) integrating it with other marketing and sales efforts such as direct mail, the field sales force, or trade journal ads; (2) deciding on the major use to which the telesales team will be put; and (3) managing the telesales operation effectively, usually a different challenge from other types of sales management.

Integrating Telesales With Other Marketing Tools

Those companies that have made teleselling work for them almost invariably use it in some combination with either direct mail or another advertising media such as a print ad. It is also often combined with in-person outside selling. For instance, Skyway Freight Systems, which provides freight and air trucking services, use two techniques to integrate teleselling with advertising. It either does a direct mailing and then follows up on leads generated using telesales people, who further qualify interest or close orders; or it uses teleselling to do cold canvassing by inquiring about a prospect's interest in receiving sales literature, which it then follows up with mailings. Skyway's use of these two systems of mail-phone or phone-mail boosted its sales in 1987 by almost $2 million. Transamerica Insurance supports its independent insurance agent network with qualified leads from a teleselling center.

A telesales operation is usually more acceptable to field salespeople if it is strictly a win-win adjunct to their own sales efforts, for instance, when telesales assistance frees them to do what they do best—namely concentrate on big accounts where face-to-face sales presentations are required. But when telesales organizations compete, instead of cooperate, with outside reps, conflict is assured and suboptimization of total efforts is quite probable.

A British Telesales Success Story

In the United Kingdom, Thorm-A-Stor,[8] a double-glazing window manufacturer, uses over three hundred telesales personnel to make cold canvas calls to find couples interested in storm windows who have not as yet decided which company to purchase from. These telesales personnel are tightly scripted and do not attempt to actually sell anything. They merely determine whether prospects would like a free quotation on new storm windows from one of the company's four hundred outside sales reps across England. If the prospect says no, they say, "Sorry to have bothered you." If the prospect says yes, the telesales person sets a convenient time for a face-to-face appointment with an outside rep. Telephone calls never last more than two minutes.

The success rate? One in twenty calls produces a prospect, and ten of these twenty eventually buy from the outside sales reps. This huge three-hundred-person telesales effort had made Thorm-A-Stor the third largest company in all of the United Kingdom in this fragmented industry.

Teleselling at Thorm-A-Stor is very tightly controlled. No calls are made after 9 P.M. at night. Complete courtesy is an ironclad rule. Brevity is a must. And appointments are always reconfirmed by the telesales group before they occur to assure that the time is still convenient for prospects to keep. If not, the telesales force backs off rather than asking for another time, because Thorm-A-Stor has found that this tactic is considered pushy. Many times those not wanting to follow through on appointments have merely had second thoughts about purchase and don't wish to say so directly to the caller.

Teleselling integration with outside selling has made Thorm-A-Stor the fastest-growing company in its industry. The president motivates his telesales personnel with bonus-based pay plans, where one third of earned income is based on results measured against forecast for the area (so different local sales potentials can be factored into the pay plan). Recognition awards of various kinds are provided. Telesales reps work part-time, in teams, and get to know their peers very well—developing local camaraderie with each other and the Thorm-A-Stor outside local rep in the territory.

Because its telesales and local reps are well-known in their local areas, they do their utmost to be honest with prospective buyers. Any negative word-of-mouth referrals about them would certainly damage their market reputation and credibility very quickly. Thorm-A-Stor is one of the United Kingdom's most innovative manufacturers, known for following up its sales promises with top-quality products.

Sorting Out Telesales Objectives

Telesales organizations can usually be categorized on the basis of their function: whether they are set up to generate orders or to perform only a partial part of the selling job, such as qualifying a prospect, announcing a new product promotion, or soliciting a lead.

Order Closing

Typically, orders are closed over the phone by companies that have an existing customer base and wish to trigger repeat sales or to upgrade order sizes, such as magazine publishers renewing subscriptions or copier companies trying to get add-on orders for copy paper, toner, or other sundries. Digital Equipment's Accessories and Supplies Group use fourteen telemarketers to handle phone orders for supplies from nine thousand customers.

J. Fegely and Sons of Pottstown, Pennsylvania, is a distributor that uses six full-time telemarketers to generate $2 million (two thousand accounts) of its $10 million in annual sales. Fegely telesells common maintenance repair and operating supplies for machine shops or metal fabricating operations.[9]

A telesales group might be asked to convince marginal accounts that buy little annual volume to place their orders by phone because the company cannot afford to make in-person calls. For example, A. B. Dick converted over 104,000 companies to telephone ordering because they each purchased only $200 in annual supplies and couldn't be serviced economically any other way. In Canada, GWG, a jean manufacturer, converted small retailers with low-volume purchases to ordering by phone. GWG's sales increased by over a million dollars in the first year from these twelve hundred small accounts, which couldn't be covered any other way except by telephone.

Telemarketing vs. Teleselling

When an organization uses the telephone to mostly promote products, sales demonstrations, or to qualify customers, it is engaged in tele*marketing* as opposed to teleselling.

The telemarketing group performs a sales qualification,

or prospecting, role for the company. Orders are then closed by a separate face-to-face sales force. For instance, NCR and Bell & Howell use telemarketers to drum up interest in free equipment demos at customers' premises or at big trade shows. A large midwestern machine toolmaker uses telemarketers to follow up on marketing literature requests received from prospects responding to trade journal ads. In every case, the telemarketers, unlike telesales personnel, are not measured directly for sales results obtained from customer call activity.

Toll-Free 800 Numbers

Toll-free 800 numbers are used extensively as a telemarketing tool to provide direct customer contact. In one survey of four hundred U.S. companies, conducted by the Society of Consumer Affairs Professionals in Business, 50 percent of companies were using toll-free service lines for customers, up from 38 percent only five years earlier. So many companies see such 800 customer service lines as strategic methods of consumer feedback. Many companies such as Pillsbury and Procter and Gamble receive feedback from customers on 800 numbers about new product uses or product problems. Johnson & Johnson receives over thirty thousand calls in Canada alone on its toll-free 800 numbers. Customers ask all sorts of questions about Johnson & Johnson's products. Johnson & Johnson answers all questions, or if calls come in during off-hours, it records the messages and answers queries first thing the following morning.

Use of 800 numbers allows companies a direct link to customer feedback, which in turn can be fed back to the sales force. When Pillsbury Canada received complaints about the taste of its new microwavable pizza, it stopped production, altered the recipe somewhat, and notified its sales force to stop pushing the old product, all in the span of a few days.[10]

A company selling mail-order chain saws used telesales personnel to clarify credit card information for those who had ordered the saw but for some reason had incompletely filled in this crucial data. The company had stopped handling such requests for credit card information follow-up by mail after over 70 percent of the customers had indignantly canceled their mail orders. Use of the phone cut such cancellations to less than 15 percent.

It is essential that companies decide very early whether the phone is to be a *supplemental* sales, service, or marketing tool, or whether teleselling is to be a complete system to move prospects right from information collection to lead qualification to gaining the initial order and sustaining reorder sales.

Managing Telesales

To manage a telesales system, a company must understand all of the variables involved.

The company must manage the design of the telesales office area, provide sufficient equipment and supervision, set up work-flow routines and record-keeping systems, and ensure that all key tasks, such as scripting, are well executed. Other necessities include selecting proper lists to call, designing forms to log call results, and backing up telesales reps with order-fulfillment personnel and systems.

Communicators must be recruited, trained, fairly compensated, directed, and kept motivated. Cost control requires excellent budgeting of phone call, wage, list acquisition, space, supervision, and equipment rental costs.

In many instances it doesn't make sense for a company to set up its own telesales group. Outside services working under contract make more economic sense. This is especially true where teleselling is required for seasonal products, concentrated sales blitzes on new products, or special one-time promotions.

Where teleselling is done by the company itself, a separate profit loss statement for the activity must be generated so that management can see both the costs and the benefits of this new function. This is the only way to determine whether the function as a stand-alone is paying its own way or is a cost center adjunct to the total selling effort.

If the company doesn't document benefits, all that management will see is higher expenses. Telesales is a powerful way to retain accounts or cover marginal accounts, thus freeing the face-to-face reps for larger accounts and fewer problem-solving calls (since these can often be handled by telephone). But failure to measure the function, as rigorously as outside selling would be measured, hides any apparent productivity gains from management reporting.

Market-Centered Sales Groups

A large number of companies have responded to more intensive competition and pressures for improved sales-force productivity by organizing all of their sales and marketing efforts by market. An excellent example is Apple Computer Inc. of Cupertino, California.[11]

Apple dominates the education market for personal computers, with large shares in both the kindergarten to grade 12 segment of the market and the higher education market, in colleges and professional schools. Such a market-centered organization has paid off for Apple in growth and profits. Apple's total sales in 1987 were up 40 percent to $2.7 billion and its profits were up 41 percent to $217 million.

Apple's thrust combines very targeted marketing and a specialist "education" sales force. Apple provides significant price discounts and sells direct via both university bookstores and special-events marketing. At the University of Michigan, Apple sold over two thousand Macintoshes to both students and faculty at a large campus sale in February of 1988. Apple advertises in education journals and has developed software for educators for both teaching subjects and handling administration. Apple's sales force calls exclusively on the various user segments within education, from teachers with classroom applications to administrators with office-work applications. Its account executives provide considerable in-class hands-on demonstrations for teachers as well as students. The reps also man booths at the large events aimed at educators—both "Applefest" and "MacWorld" trade shows.

The size of Apple's dedicated education sales force is larger than most American book publishers, because the company concentrates on over three thousand universities and even more local school boards.

Apple's market-centered sales strategy is being extended to a new fast-growth market for desktop publishing. Its sales force is helping develop new desktop publishing uses for everyone from state and local government officials (who find the Macintosh great for filing local zoning maps) to lawyers (who use the Macintosh to file their briefs). Apple's market-centered organization is helping expand the total desktop publishing market from $600 million in 1987 (all competitors) to estimates of over a billion dollars by 1991. Such market-centered sales specialization frequently expands the total market for products because the strong market focus leverages up total applications. Word of mouth among potential market users recommending the new product is positively increased.

The Components of Vertical Sales Specialization

In order to be successful with a niche-targeted sales organization, a number of components must fit together. As the Apple case illustrates, the marketing strategy must be very focused with specifically targeted pricing, advertising media selection, trade shows, and distribution decisions (such as Apple selling to students through bookstores instead of its Apple dealers, and selling to administrators *directly* instead of through a reseller). On the sales side of the coin, the following tactics are usually found in successful niche-sales organizations:

Aids and Literature

• Sales aids are customized to fit the target buyers. For example, literature is written in the language of the respective users, and cost/benefit stories are customized to them.

• Third-party testimonials and application success stories are relevant to the users and allow the target segment to identify immediately with circumstances and problems similar to their own.

Training and Sales Techniques

• The training of the sales reps is tailored; they are taught and coached on presenting features and benefits relevant to different target segments. Reps get on the same wavelength as the prospects they sell to. IBM has 75 percent of its reps trained as specialists in one market or another.

• End users are often sold to in groups, using a "seminar sell" approach tailored to their needs. For instance, Apple's reps selling desktop publishing use one sales seminar for engineers with CAD-CAM design tie-in needs, and another if the end users are advertising artists with graphic display needs for creative layouts.

• Specialized sales reps frequently join trade associations to which target customers also belong. For example, a manufacturer of products sold to building contractors would join associations whose membership includes these builders.

• Sales reps often take courses targeted at their *user* customers in order to understand their customers' orientations and concerns. For example, a sales organization selling products to a police force could send its reps to take night school courses at a local police college. A sales force selling equipment to pulp and paper companies might enroll its reps in courses sponsored by the Pulp and Paper Institute. The sales force of a manufacturer targeting the electronics industry might require its reps to take some electronic technology or electrical engineering courses at a university or junior college nearby.

"Contact" Programs and Compensation Plans

• Successful vertical sales organizations often have extensive "contact" programs with customers at *three levels:* the sales rep/user customer level; the sales manager/user customer middle-management level (purchasing or department managers); and the vice-president of sales/user-customer executive level. In this way the commitment to the segment runs through and through the vertical sales-directed organization.

• Since vertical sales organizations are often oriented to market development activities, sales commissions and incentives must be structured to reward this often time-consuming activity. Thus, "commission only" type schemes are discarded in favor of compensation plans that recognize new account successes and growth in "up-selling" important accounts with multiple order placements. Salary and bonuses tied to growth by account or segment make much more sense.

Sales Time and Sales Approaches by City

Sales time is frequently allocated, in vertical sales organizations, to capture the support of *younger* user customers. For instance, a medical products manufacturer targeted to surgeons or nurses spends considerable time raising both awareness and the company's profile at nursing schools and medical schools (despite the fact that the new nurse or newly graduating surgeon is not necessarily an immediate big consumer of the company's products). Makers of CAD-CAM equipment make numerous presentations to new engineers and architects at college. One favorite tactic is to sponsor a scholarship for some worthy student and gain publicity for the sales organization in this way.

Because vertical sales organizations are often spread across the nation, many astute companies tailor their sales approaches geographically. IBM does this by sales branch in the United States, targeting specific markets such as military or naval bases. Where markets are not as dispersed, such as the automotive makers in Detroit or the aerospace industry in Texas and Seattle, companies often set up their vertical sales groups at the geographic center of such markets.

Accounting and Communications

Sales groups that are market centered must have sales reports and profit and loss statements produced from accounting *by market* (instead of by product line, as is usual in most companies). In addition to accounting reports, a specialized market-centered organization needs extensive computer and communications hook-ups with its customers. For example, companies concentrating on selling to auto makers in Detroit use facsimile transmission and electronic data interface extensively for invoicing, ordering, exchanging specifications, arranging key meetings, sorting out application problems, or placing special demands on each other (order expedites, orders for custom nonstandard items, and advance notice of changes to planned order shipping).

Vertical sales organizations do not necessarily have to be run from the head office, nor do they have to be headed by marketing personnel. At PPG Industries, Fibre Glass Reinforcement Product Division, four regional managers were given the mandate in different geographic regions to investigate emerging sales opportunities in specialized key industries such as automotive makers. These sales managers organized interdisciplinary teams comprised of sales reps and both marketing and technical personnel to adapt PPG's technologies for new products required of these major end-user target customers.

Internal Inertia

Despite the fact that excellent tools and training can be put in place to refocus sales reps on vertical markets instead of products, the transition still takes time. The field sales force has to change its way of thinking. One manufacturer whose reps sold centrifuges and who were chemical engineers by training, found it took years to reorient these reps to understand the needs of particular industries such as food or mineral processors. The sales vice-president said it was "like turning an aircraft carrier around, a lot slower and more awkward than we thought before we started the program."

A Sales Specialization Success Story

H. B. Fuller is an excellent example of a company that moved its sales reps into specialized selling by industry with dramatically improved results. Fuller manufactures more than one thousand types of adhesives for one hundred different industries. Traditionally it organized sales reps by territory, asking them to service all types of accounts and know the properties, peculiarities, and applications of all its adhesives. This created two problems. First, Fuller reps often sold to unprofitable small accounts simply because these were local businesses in their territories. Second, the reps never knew enough about the specialized needs of large adhesive-consuming industries to become credible experts. In 1982 Fuller's chief executive, Tony Andersen, reassigned reps to become specialists for large user industries such as graphic arts, where book gluing requires a deep knowledge of printer and magazine-publisher binding systems.

While customer service suffered slightly initially because industry knowledge took time to learn, by 1988 sales doubled and Fuller's return on equity improved. Customers began to recognize that Fuller really knew their needs, and responded favorably by giving Fuller a bigger share of their purchases.

National (or Global) Account Managers

National account management is another corporate response to increased competition and the need for higher-yield sales productivity. As one sales executive has said succinctly, "Our scorecard in the sales operation is the value of bookings of our services/products per sales rep. On average, we have seen about 40 percent higher yield across key accounts, based on the influence of the national account program."

National account management recognizes that certain very large accounts are of strategic importance to the company. Failure to coordinate and channel the most sophisticated sales and marketing approaches toward these accounts represents lost opportunity and suboptimization of sales efforts. Companies vary in their orientation toward national accounts. Some focus their efforts on key distributors or wholesalers, such as Becton Dickinson. Becton Dickinson set up four "account business managers" to leverage its effectiveness with huge national multibranch distributors whose sales cut across the traditional regional sales organization Becton Dickinson had in place. These account business managers work hand in glove with regional sales managers to "sell the company" to such powerful distributors, using such methods as tailoring a variety of sales and marketing tools for the distributors, from lead generation programs and distributor sales incentive contests to cooperative advertising plans that provide distributors with camera-ready artwork for their own direct mailings.

National Account Programs and Retailers

At companies selling to retailers, usually at the vice-presidential level, such as Campbell Soup, the national account manager focuses on the giants such as Safeway. A key part of the vice-president's job is to hold semiannual business reviews with these retailers, covering Campbell's total business with them, including special focus on its merchandising allowances, advertising activities, stocking practices, and backhaul freight programs. Campbell contrasts all of these elements with those of its soup competitors, as a way of demonstrating Campbell's commitment to the account. The vice-president of national accounts is very instrumental at handling complaints not resolved at the field sales rep level and communicating any new changes in Campbell's selling terms or allowances for spoilage.

At manufacturer's such as Norton, a maker of industrial abrasives, or at Moore Corporation, a manufacturer of business forms, national accounts represent customers with multiple factories and corporate-level purchasing. Such customers are looking more and more for sole supplier relationships to reduce their total costs of doing business with multiple vendors across the country. The national account manager becomes the coordinator of team selling to these complex accounts where both multilevel sales contacts and extensive vertical industry market knowledge (about a customer's industry) are required. Frequently the national account manager negotiates national agreements with these giant accounts, covering prices, extra services offered (provision of just-in-time inventory or extra engineering supports), and how the account will be handled by appointed distributors.

Key Success Factors in National Account Programs

Converting important national accounts from customers into "clients" with long-term working relationships with the company is not easy.[12]

Consider, for example, the case of General Electric, which operates fourteen different businesses. When GE wanted to convince General Motors to give it all of the electrical business at its new Saturn plant, GE pulled together a forty-person team from its divisions to land the account. The team had to include engineers, sales representatives, and service personnel from its diverse divisions including power systems and plastics. An all-out effort had to be focused under a senior vice-president to negotiate specifications and pricing for myriad GE products, from transformers to motor controls. GE began by making its intentions known at the highest levels at General Motors—the office of Chairman Roger Smith. The task took two years of coordinated plant tours between General Motors' engineers and purchasing people and the GE sales, production, and order-processing personnel.[13]

Experience has shown that a few key factors usually determine whether a national account management program will be a success.

Selection of the Person to Head a National Account Function

The selection of the right person to handle national accounts is critical. The desired qualifications of excellent national account managers usually include a long and successful career in the field sales force (about twenty years). In addition the individual has extensive knowledge of the marketplace generally, his or her company and its capabilities, and often specific knowledge of the accounts likely to be nominated for national account status. Because of such experience and knowledge, the individual is respected both inside and outside the company. The person needs four key skills: excellent negotiation skills to bargain on financial terms with accounts; strong sales presentation skills to relate the company's capabilities to the customer; interpersonal skills to maintain multiple contacts in the hierarchy at the customer company; and research skills to find and profile account needs for the marketing organization to design programs that benefit the account. As individuals gain experience handling national accounts, they often become expert in determining how *their client customers* make investment decisions, planning decisions, and decisions on enhanced productivity within their companies.

Providing Authority, Rewards, and Resources to Make National Account Management Work

If the company has picked the right person to head a national account program, it must integrate this activity into its overall sales organization and structure the national account manager's activities to produce measurable results.

To integrate the national account manager, the regular regional sales organizations must be convinced of the need for such a position and involved in defining the responsibilities of the position. One recent survey of 150 national account managers reported in *Business Marketing* magazine showed that more than a quarter of their time can be spent trying to garner support *internally* for their programs. The national account manager must regularly report on presentations and communications being made with key national accounts, and how these tactics are paying off for the company. In many instances it makes sense for the sales credit (for increased business done with national accounts) to be prorated and *shared* with regional managers and sales reps in whose territory the national accounts reside. This reduces harmful internal competition between the national account manager and the sales force, who must assist him or her in achieving sales plan goals with these key accounts.

Strong vs. Limited Mandates

Senior management must confer on the national account manager the authority to carry out his or her mandate, whether it is limited or all-encompassing. A limited mandate involves assigning a national account manager as a staff executive to coordinate and monitor the activities of all the company's sales and service resources that deal with strategically important customers. A stronger mandate involves appointing the national account manager as the line executive with direct responsibility to grow the sales and profits from national accounts, utilizing all the marketing, sales, and service resources in the company to ensure this. With line authority, the national account manager would likely have responsibility to sign annual contracts with national accounts for prices, annual expected purchase volumes, and additional promised services such as expedited complaint resolution, custom engineering support, special delivery services, unique packaging, made-to-order order assortments, and one-of-a-kind order-handling routines.

Some companies insist that their national account managers prepare business plans by specific account. A plan usually details the current amount of business done with the account, and an analysis of the account's strengths and weaknesses and potential purchases. This can provide fertile ideas for improvements to assist the account. For instance, one company analyzed a national account's abilities to forecast its own needs by week and month. The analysis showed that the account was very poor at forecasting its own material volume requirements. As a result the account was creating service problems for the national account manager's inventory control people. The national account manager therefore asked the large account if it would allow the vendor to manage the entire order/demand process for purchased products, thereby assuring better supply availability. The account readily agreed to do this. Service improved markedly and both parties gained. The account had fewer out-of stocks, and the vendor smoothed its demand scheduling and lowered the amount of safety stock it carried in inventory because of poor needs forecasting.

An account-specific plan might include the following headings (for an industrial market):

1. Account profile, e.g., buying history, our share of accounts business
2. Account's strengths/weaknesses
3. Strategies we will pursue with account:

   - Pricing
   - Delivery
   - Sales mix of items
   - Services
   - Quality control
   - New product introductions
   - Communications/problem-solving forums
   - Packaging

4. Overall target share of account and target profitability

An account-specific strategy for a large target retailer account would have different subheads under "strategies" such as:

   - Promotions to be run/Timing
   - Display supports
   - Dealing and sell-in programs
   - Media plan/Co-op ads
   - Special prices
   - Training for store staff
   - Returned goods (end of season)

In either a staff or line role, the national account manager's responsibilities must be clear to both senior managers in the company who have established the position and to those who must assist the national account manager in implementing any plans.

It's vital that everyone know whether the national account manager is to be an orchestra leader for others, with only dotted-line authority for coordinating mutual efforts to boost business with these critical accounts (and possibly making selected key presentations to them), or whether the national account manager has direct controlling authority over all activities that go on at such major customers.

The Selection of Critical Accounts

Assuming the position's mandate is clear, a company can set to work to identify which accounts require specialized attention, how many such accounts can be handled by the national account manager (and staff), and what sort of account profiles and results reporting are required to monitor progress and account potentials. In many companies, fewer than ten national accounts are handled by a national account manager; in others the numbers are larger (thirty to fifty accounts).

In every case, determining *who* deserves national account treatment requires some definition. A selected target company often offers great sales potential in absolute dollars and as a percent of its total sales. It usually has multiple purchase sites cutting across sales regions. It offers above-average profit possibilities, buys centrally for disparate geographic locations, and is considered a leader in its industry. Great judgment and diplomacy are needed to decide who gets national account status; without clear standards to decide this, the company may be beseiged by customer requests for special pricing and services. A good data base needs to be set up for all accounts granted national status, in order to capture all their buying influences, contacts, product usages, and purchasing procedures. Actual sales results should round out the data base, to provide quarterly progress reports and detailed breakdowns of sales according to factory site and specific product. These can then be compared to target sales levels and actual volumes sold in prior quarters, to decide whether the national account program is working to generate incremental business.

Setting up such a system is difficult, because many companies gear computer systems for accounting rather than marketing. Putting a tracking program by account in place is therefore not always straightforward nor simple. For example, if a company sells some of its products directly to a national account and some products through an appointed distributor, its own sales records, based on invoices, show only the direct account purchases. The others are hidden in purchases by its assigned distributor, which could include the distributor's purchases for a multitude of accounts (not just the national account).

The national account manager should publicize key-account activities and ongoing results in company newsletters and to accounts visited in the field, and have sales reps support this effort. The publicity provides high visibility for the national account manager across the company, both functionally and geographically.

National Account Management Results

Over 185 national account managers attended the National Account Marketing Association's 1988 annual meeting in San Diego—an increase of 30 percent in attendance over the previous year. Over seventy-eight of the attendees were brand new to the field. The belief in national account management is therefore clearly growing. Large, medium, and even relatively small companies are benefiting from such programs. A very large firm such as Occidental Chemical Company have appointed national account managers to handle multinational customers with one-stop shopping on chlorine and sodium hydroxide products. Such customers now account for almost $1 billion of Occidental's total $2.8 billion in sales.

A medium-size company such as Petrolite Corporation (St. Louis), a $28 million industrial chemical maker, have eighteen huge corporate accounts that comprise 60 percent of their sales volume. And by using national account management, Petrolite has increased sales to such giant customers by 20 percent. Petrolite moved sales to one key oil company account from $100,000 to $1 million in just two years with its major-account sales emphasis.

Even small companies such as the Milwaukee-based Kelley Company, a leading dock equipment manufacturer, became interested in national accounts in 1983. Thereafter, it boosted the importance of such accounts in its sales mix from 11.5 percent in 1983 to 15 percent in 1988.

The success formula for all these companies continues to be combining national account management programs with vertical marketing knowledge (systems solutions for customers) in an organized, coordinated way. Even service-providing companies such as Dun and Bradstreet and Automatic Data Processing Inc. are demonstrating outstanding results from national account organizations. National account management as a sales technique therefore works for both manufacturers and service providers, whether accounts are resellers or end users. The key is to staff the function properly, provide it with strong upper-management support and understanding, and then integrate it successfully with the rest of the mainstream sales organization. Successful integration requires clear communication of the national account functions mandate, appropriate reward sharing among the salespeople involved, and sound management of the new function's forecasting, contract pricing, and services and progress reporting.

Summary

Competitors, by squeezing margins in many industries, are forcing sales managements to look for heightened productivity. This has spawned efforts to reduce sales costs and/or leverage sales results by industry or account. The result has been energetic initiatives by sales organizations to reorganize using inside telesales people, market-centered sales reps, or national account managers. Whole new challenges and career paths are therefore open to territory reps. New skills must be learned and new approaches to customers tried, including account- or industry-specific planning on a more in-depth basis. Each form of sales specialization presents its own unique challenges, but common to all three is the need to integrate multiple selling mix options, because most companies use several options simultaneously (telephone selling to small accounts, territory reps in some regions, market specialist reps in some regions, and national account managers for giant customers). The expanded selling mix requires a company to alter supports by rep specialist, to set different goals/targets by method of selling, and to appraise results differentially according to selling option.

Further Readings

Bencil, Richard L. "Building a Telemarketing Blueprint." *Sales and Marketing Management Canada* (September 1988), pp. 24–25.

Bertrand, Kate. "Customer Demands Ignite National Account Marketing." *Business Marketing* (July 1988), p. 36.

———. "National Account Marketing." *Business Marketing* (November 1987), pp. 43–64.

Cardillo Platzer, Linda. "Managing National Accounts." *Conference Board Report* No. 850, 1984.

Coppett, John, and R. D. Voorhess. "Telemarketing: Supplement to Field Sales." *Industrial Marketing Management* 14 (August 1985), pp. 214–215.

Cordoza, Richard, and Shannon Shipp. "New Selling Methods are Changing Industrial Sales Management." *Business Horizons* (September–October 1987), pp. 23–28.

Hanan, Mack. "Reorganize Your Company Around Its Markets." *Harvard Business Review* (November–December 1974), pp. 63–74.

Hlavacek, J. D., and B. C. Ames. "Segmenting Business Markets." In their book *Managerial Marketing for Industrial Firms* (New York: Random House, 1984), pp. 92–109.

Hunter, Michael. "Getting Started in National Account Marketing." *Business Marketing* (November 1987), pp. 61–64.

Liswood, Laura A. "Once You've Got 'Em Never Let 'Em Go." *Sales and Marketing Management* (November 1987), pp. 73–75. An article on "customer retention" strategies.

"National Account Marketers Want More Support." *Business Marketing* (August 1989), p. 26.

Rogers, R., and V. Chamberlain III. *National Account Marketing Handbook.* New York: AMACOM, 1981.

Roman, Murray. *Telephone Marketing.* New York: McGraw-Hill, 1976.

Shapiro, Benson, and R. Moriarty. "Organizing the National Account Force." *Marketing Science Institute Report* No. 84-101, 1984.

Shipp, Shannon, K. Roering, and R. Cardoza. "Implementing a New Selling Mix." *Journal of Business and Industrial Marketing* 3, 2 (Summer 1988), pp. 55–63.

Steckel, Robert. *Profitable Telephone Sales Operations.* New York: Arco Publishing, 1975.

Sutton, Howard. "Rethinking the Company's Selling and Distribution Channels." *Conference Board Report* No. 885, 1986, especially section on sales force specialization, pp. 2–3.

Chapter 3

The Effects of
Changing Distribution
on the Sales Game

Consider what an enviable position distributors are in to make changes in the course of their businesses. Their assets are mainly liquid—mainly inventories and receivables. They don't own Taj Mahal real estate or expensive single purpose machinery. They are not large corporations with bulging standard procedure manuals.

—Robert Clifton
Editor, *Industrial Distribution*
November 1988

Chapter 1 outlines changes in a variety of markets and discusses how each of these are affecting the sales rep. Sales organizations are being transformed into selling services instead of products—selling "solutions" to end customers besieged by multiple vendor choices—and selling in teams, with a "higher order" of professionalism required across all selling skills. As products lose differentiation, selling itself is now separating rivals and providing competitive distinctiveness and "value-added" to customers.

Chapter 2 outlines how competitive shifts in markets are putting pressure on margins and in turn forcing sales reps to specialize by vertical market and national account or to shed some smaller accounts to more efficient telesales organizations. Thus customer changes are forcing more teamwork and professionalism on sales reps, while competitive pressure is leading to new organizational forms that enhance sales productivity.

But customer and competitor changes are only two of the compelling forces altering the selling game. A third dynamic factor in the sales environment is the changing distribution channel landscape. Wholesalers, retailers, and other major types of middlemen such as agents are undergoing rapid transformations that are affecting both sales reps who sell *for them* and suppliers' sales reps who sell *to them*.

Changes in Wholesalers and Distributors

Wholesalers and distributors are changing in a multitude of specific ways, which can be summarized into three "macro" changes. First, wholesalers and distributors are growing in size, geographic influence, and importance.

Second, wholesalers and distributors are increasing in their sophistication.

Finally, many distributors are specializing in high-tech markets, for instance, selling systems to help factories automate their production lines to gain productivity, quality, and output flexibility. A distributor such as Miller and Dietz, in Frazer, Pennsylvania, sells programmable controllers that assist its manufacturing customers in solving efficiency problems. This highly specialized company is equipped to sell complete systems of computer hardware, system tools such as sensors and actuators, and application software. Commitments to specialization, though expensive, provide such distributors with a competitive edge. For instance, Miller-Knapp Electronic, in Edison, New Jersey, had to invest in a $150,000 training center for its own customers and staff. The classroom facility includes computer workstations and machine interface demos to train users and sales reps about programmable controllers, the company's bread-and-butter line of products.

Each of these macrochanges confers increased power and credibility to the wholesaler or distributor.

Figure 3-1 illustrates the concept.

Distributor/Wholesaler Size and Scope

The Distribution Research and Education Foundation, in an extensive study of wholesalers and distributors, documented current and anticipated future changes in their operations. One of the major findings is that the largest wholesalers are getting even bigger, as they acquire the medium-size wholesalers over time. Mergers and buyouts are creating larger wholesaler companies, as the large wholesalers seek to spread overheads over more volume and discover that adding geographic branches or new market areas can be more productively accomplished through acquisition than through starting from scratch. Many family-owned, medium-size wholesaler companies, lacking an heir to the founder, are often open to the idea of selling the business and cashing out. Wholesaler buyouts will cut the number of American wholesalers by 25 percent by the year 1995. For example, The Summers Group, an electrical distributor, had sales of $240 million in 1986. By 1988, through acquisition, its sales reached $500 million, more than double its 1986 volume.

As the importance of truly huge wholesalers grows, manufacturers are putting more business through them.

Direct selling is becoming prohibitively expensive for many manufacturers, as margins are squeezed by more global rivals. A case in point is the copier market, where companies today rely much more on dealers than they did in the past. The same scenario is also occurring in the market for fax equipment and microcomputers, where price declines have forced manufacturers to employ lower-cost sales channels than direct selling. The amount of business conducted through wholesalers of one kind or another is forecasted to grow from 59 percent of all American economic activity in 1987 to 63 percent by 1992. And not all of this extra distributor selling is confined to American-made prod-

Figure 3-1. How the power and credibility of wholesalers is increasing.

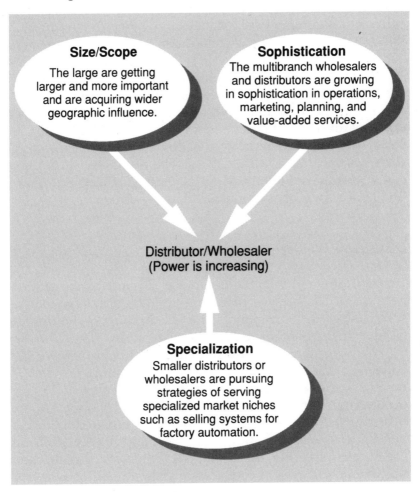

ucts. The Distribution Research and Education Foundation study forecasts the percentage of wholesaler total purchases from foreign suppliers to grow from 10 percent in 1987 to 18 percent by 1995.

In addition, the use of independent manufacturers' agents as a channel of distribution for mature products is declining over time. This is forecasted to continue because such agents do not offer just-in-time logistical service on many commonplace items to customers. (Most agents do not inventory or invoice customers for sale; they merely arrange sales on a manufacturer's behalf and collect a commission for doing this.) For new technology products, agents will continue to perform a valuable role in the economy.

A considerable number of wholesalers and distributors are huge national or even international companies, the size of Fortune 500 manufacturers. For instance, W. W. Grainger operates over 300 branches and does over $1.5 billion in sales per year. Other large distributor companies include Bearings Inc., Motion Industries, The Summers Group, Arrow Electronics, Flemming Foods, Greybar Electric, Noland Co., McKeeson Corporation, and Lawson Products.

Distributor/Wholesaler Sophistication

Distributors' and wholesalers' power is increasing not only because of the growth of giants and the shake-out of the small and mid-size regionals, but also because of their much greater business management sophistication.

They are making extensive investments in hiring more college-educated staff and acquiring more computers to better manage warehouses, truck fleets, receivables, and order processing. For instance, in warehousing, wholesalers are investing heavily in bar code scanners, automated material-handling systems, robotics, flow racks, and conveyors. Their use of telemarketing, electronic data interface (linking their customers' computers to theirs), facsimile equipment, and desktop publishing (for catalog and direct-mail advertising insert preparation) is growing rapidly.

It is estimated that over 45 percent of all orders between distributors and customers will use high-tech communication by 1995, compared to only 9 percent of such orders in 1987. For instance, Noland Co., a diversified distributor with over $400 million in sales, lets its 35,000 customers hookup to its computer for automated purchasing twenty-four hours a day. Computer investments allow great staff productivity gains because distributor personnel can do on-line credit checks on orders, monitor buying preferences of key accounts, and program in price or product changes much faster than they could manually. American distributors with computers had a 33 percent better return on investment in 1987 than did distributors still using manual systems.

As a result of growing business and operational sophistication, wholesalers are offering all kinds of value-added services or are specializing more by market to increase their utility in specific vertical markets to their customers. R. S. Hughes of California, a specialized distributor of adhesives, grew from five branches in 1961 to twenty by concentrating on only the adhesives market niche. It can act as a value-added consultant on adhesives with its customers. The true test of whether increasing wholesaler or distributor sophistication is beneficial, however, is whether it pays off for the middleman's customers—in reduced costs, increased efficiency, or a way for the customer to increase its prices or improve its products. Some food service wholesalers have combined their increased sophistication in computers with their knowledge of their food service customers' sales. They offer computerized programs that help these food service companies provide better forecasts of food usage according to institution. The better forecast service allows the food service caterers to save money on purchases and improve their profits.

High-tech distributors of factory automation equipment help their customers reduce the need for additional factory labor or avoid adding extra factory capacity by increasing the customer's capacity yield by means of new technology. The manufacturer can then be more cost competitive and often offer higher consistent quality products at premium pricing.

The degree of distributor/wholesaler sophistication is also apparent in the use of more strategic planning and the appointment of younger, professionally trained chief executive officers.

Value-Added Services

As wholesalers and distributors grow in sophistication, a great many are jumping into new value-added services.

Wholesalers have added such services at an ever prolif-erating rate in six areas, as illustrated in Figure 3-2.

• *A technical* value-added service offered by a whole-saler or distributor could be equipment repair or engineer-ing-design services. A wholesaler such as McNaughton-McKay, which markets automation and high-tech-process control equipment (test instruments, controls, software, and industrial computers), offers extensive custom engineering services from graduate electrical engineers on its staff. Mc-Naughton-McKay put system components together to offer a manufacturer a turnkey factory automation system.

• *Logistical transactional services* include services such as contract-supply-just-in-time delivery. Cameron & Barkley Co., a large U.S. distributor, was awarded all of General Electric's U.S. appliance parts business (a $10 million con-tract) because it could provide such just-in-time service including electronic order hookups for the on-line exchange of orders, releases, advance shipping notices, and invoices.

• *Financial services* include leasing or rental programs such as those offered by office equipment wholesalers who rent furniture to end users.

• Food service wholesalers provide restaurants with *value-added operations help* with designs for restaurants and kitchen layouts that optimize food handling and preparation.

• *Educational* services that wholesalers often opt for include providing their customers with hands-on operator training for their products or educational seminars about product selection. General Industrial Supply, a Texas-based industrial products distributor, offers ten to twenty courses about product applications to their user accounts.

Changes Among Retailers

Changes in the retail scene are as dramatic as those among wholesalers or distributors.

Retailing chains are growing in power and buying clout as they buy out independents in many retailing classes of

Figure 3-2. Wholesaler/distributor value-added services by type.

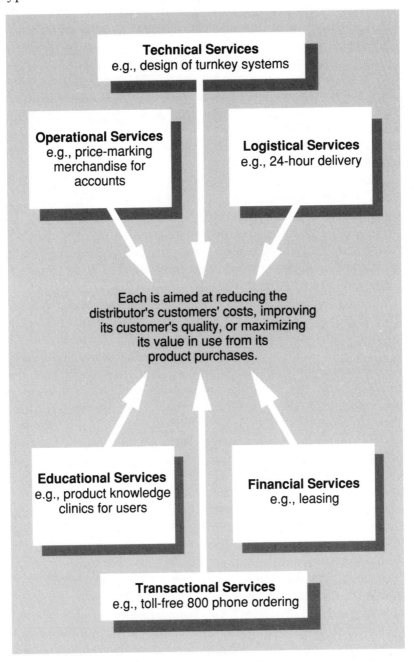

trade. For instance, in the American market, the percentage of all grocery products sold by the top five grocery chain stores has gone from *40* percent in 1983 to *48* percent in 1988. This represents a 20 percent power boost in volumes purchased per giant chain!

This same phenomenon of national chain store power is being played out in a variety of retail trade classes from drugstores (where regionals are being bought up by nationals) to discount stores (where Wal-Mart stores and K Mart are growing their influence) to the more traditional preserves of independents such as sporting goods, jewelry, and home building center stores.

Chains such as Circuit City stores, Toys R Us, Rite Aid, The Limited, Nordstroms, and others are getting increasingly big pieces of their specialty retail markets. Toys R Us is closing in on its goal of selling 40 percent of all toys in the United States by 1990. And some retailers who have grown in stature have done so on a global basis, such as Ikea, the huge Swedish furniture retailer.

The power ascendency is attributable not solely to numbers of stores and annual volumes purchased, but also to the retailers' strong success with private label brands, which often outsell branded national manufacturers' products. Sears's television set sales now exceed those of Sony, and the Sears line of Craftsman tools and Kenmore appliances is on a par with brands such as Black and Decker, Stanley Tool, and General Electric.

The knowledge chains have about end-customer buying preferences often exceeds that of manufacturers because the chain stores have integrated their cash registers with their inventory control systems. A retailer instantly knows the shelf movements and share-of-shelf by product line, while manufacturers must pay for such data from companies like A. C. Nielsen. It is therefore difficult for manufacturers to sell to retailers, who often know more then they do about what appeals to the end customers for brand-name product promotions. This is true even though the manufacturers actually make the products in question. No doubt Sears known more about the pricing, preferred timing, and appealing features of automatic garage-door openers than do suppliers who dominate this business, such as Stanley Tool. The reason is simple: Sears gets its market research *by the hour*, not after many weeks of waiting for such data from companies such as Nielsen or SAMI (Selling Areas Marketing Incorporated).

Blurring Retail Trade Classes

Consumers patronize all sorts of retailers that either didn't exist as a trade class years ago or certainly didn't sell the range of products they sell today. For instance, wholesale clubs such as the Price Club, a $3.3 billion retailer, didn't even exist a few short years ago. Today food chains sell drugstore items, drug chains sell food items, hardware stores sell auto parts, and convenience stores sell hot prepared foods. Some retail trade classes have evolved to become hybrids of once-separate types of retailers. For instance, home electronics stores now sell products such as televisions, stereos, and audio equipment as well as computers, software, cellular phones, pagers, and calculators. This represents a hybrid of stores that used to exist separately as either TV-stereo stores or computer stores.

Home building centers combine decorator products (often sold mostly in paint and wallpaper stores) with traditional lumber and building materials. Some home building chains even sell bedding and housewares—the former province of department stores. The blurring of trade classes has profound implications on the sales forces of suppliers that sell to such retailers. Sales reps must customize sales programs, promotions, deals, and planograms to fit a multitude of retail formats.

For example, computer accessories and supplies may be sold in a large discount store with lots of square footage for display but staffed by salespeople who are not computer knowledgeable. These same computers and supplies might be sold in a specialty store with much less display space but with more highly trained sales staffs who are able to assist shoppers. Obviously, the sales force selling its computer accessories to discount department stores will need sell-in programs for such retailers that emphasize packaging, display, and point-of-sales literature to act as "silent salespeople" for its lines. In the specialty stores, supplier reps can train the retail staffs and propose smaller display and floor units that accommodate the more cramped conditions.

Some changes on the retail scene require supplier reps to deal with entirely new *nonstore* channels. These include mail-order houses, catalog marketers, and TV shopping organizations. American Express is no longer just a credit card, financial services company. It sold over $500 million in mail order merchandise in 1988. The product range covers jewelry, home furnishings, electronics, art reproductions, Christmas gift items, and health/fitness products. American Express is even considering a new catalog to sell *businesses* products through the mail.

Some retail trade classes are not concerned about these indirect mail-order competitor channels. They believe they can hold their share of shopping volumes by enhancing the shopping experience with value-added services and knowledgeable sales personnel. For example, department stores are adding in-store services ranging from dental and optical clinics to microwave cooking classes. Carson Pirie Scott, a department store in Chicago, offers a complete floor of services to busy career women from hairdressing salons to fitness facilities and on-the-spot shoe repairs and dress alterations.

The Effect of All These Wholesaling and Retailing Changes on Sales Reps

The impact of wholesaler or retailer changes on sales reps is a function of perspective, which can be arrayed on a two-by-two grid.

As Figure 3-3 illustrates, the changing nature of wholesalers or distributors affects the sales personnel working *for* these companies or selling *to* them. This is also true of retailers, whose in-store salespeople are being affected by changes in retailing. The manufacturers selling *to* such retailers are also affected.

It makes sense, therefore, to detail how each participant in the distribution channel will be altered by the shifting nature of each type of middleman company.

Figure 3-3. Effects of wholesaler/retailer changes.

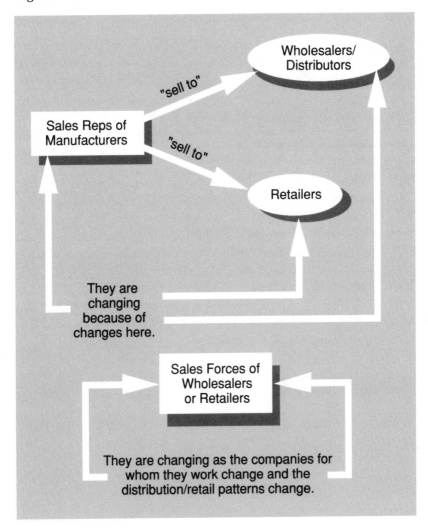

How Changing Wholesalers' Companies Are Affecting Their Own Sales Staff

As distributors grow in sophistication and size, those selling products or services for them are being affected dramatically. There are two major changes. The first is that the differences between inside sales rep tasks and outside sales rep tasks are widening. As distributors modernize their telesales and at the same time move to offer just-in-time value-added services, their inside reps will become the implementation arm of their catalog marketing and will need to be highly efficient at upgrading orders, selling repeat customers, handling medium and small accounts, and launching promotions and special deals over the telephone. Some distributors such as McMaster-Carr of Chicago conduct all their business via telemarketing and mail-order/courier delivery.

A wholesaler's outside reps will become more specialized than ever at selling value-added services such as contract systems programs to major accounts. These outside reps will need to become highly skilled at working with all the buying influences within key accounts, to maximum revenue per customer. The distributor outside reps will need to become expert on not just the products they sell to these accounts, but on the customer's business—in order to become advisors to large accounts (who will form closer partnerships with such distributors).

Distributor Reps as Problem Solvers

Hagerty Brothers Co. is a major supplier of fasteners, hand tools, abrasives, and cutting tools to Caterpillar Tractor (the construction equipment maker). Hagerty's whole sales approach is to have its salespeople act as problem solvers for Caterpillar, including getting to know and understand the needs of eight separate and different buying influences. These include purchasing people (buyers/assistant buyers); plant engineering personnel (who specify tool use for production); tool crib supervisors (who issue tools and maintain inventories of maintenance items); tool users; supervisors of production people and supervisors of maintenance personnel; production planners (who plan for future plant modernization of assembly operations); and even the plant manager (concerned with production output and both production and maintenance costs). Thus Hagerty's outside sales reps detail all these influences and readily spend two to three times a week ensuring that their tools are helping Caterpillar with its production and maintenance needs. As one purchasing official aptly stated in discussing a distributor's outside sales reps, "We don't want the sales person to walk away once a blanket purchase order is signed."[1] A distributor such as Hagerty puts the problem another way: "The days that sales people dropped off a few catalogs, took someone out to lunch and scribbled purchase orders on scratch pads are over."[2]

Distributor Reps' Educational Levels

The second big change occurring with the sales personnel of distributors and wholesalers is their need for additional education and training. Many today must receive advanced training in selling skills and be much more computer literate, since their companies are computerizing more and more parts of their operation. For instance, inside telesales reps need training to know how to close orders over the phone, to handle customer objections smoothly, and to manage their telesales time and assigned accounts. This requires courses, and coaching on subjects such as time management and "customer questioning" (where the telesales person is taught to draw customers out over the phone, so that calls lead to orders). Outside sales reps must be taught how to probe customers to discover the value-added services they desire. In this way, the outside wholesaler rep can feed information back to his company, so that such value-added service programs can be developed and offered for sale.

In some distributor companies, where the market involves selling high-tech components such as digital process control systems, the distributor salesperson must often be a graduate engineer in order to sell the *concept* of using programmable logic controllers in a potential customer's factory process. McNaughton-McKay,[3] a high-tech distributor, has fifteen graduate electrical engineers selling its automation process control equipment to its customers. These engineers must be technically trained well enough to explain automation concepts not just to project engineers at their accounts, but also to the senior managers in charge of authorizing such capital appropriation requests. As distributors move into more high-tech markets, their sales reps must have a background in software, computers, and systems, because they cannot depend on learning on the job what they need to know (as was the case in more low-tech and slower-changing markets where mechanical controls such as gears, motors, and belts could be more easily understood).

Selling to Distributors or Wholesalers

Manufacturers' sales forces selling to markedly changing distributors or wholesalers with more buying clout must teach their reps new roles. They must teach them how to become business advisors to distribution instead of mere sales personnel, because distributors are more conscious of skilled balance-sheet management, market positioning, and the need for higher quality value-added services. The distributors are sourcing from suppliers whose sales representatives can assist them not just with products, but with the entire thrust of their efforts to carve out defensible market positions and earn adequate financial returns on investments in receivables, warehouses, branches, computers, and inventories. Briggs-Weaver, a large industrial distributor, has helped many of its end customers lower their total procurement costs by astute inventory management. As a result, many of its customers have given over 100 percent of their business to Briggs-Weaver. This makes a distributor such as Briggs-Weaver more powerful and able to demand top-notch service from its manufacturing suppliers.

The manufacturers' salespeople therefore need to couple the value-added produced by their company with the desired market positioning of their appointed distributor(s).

For example, a manufacturer of a new line of wood preservatives and water repellants needed to establish its position with key regional building material wholesalers in order to get its products sold into retail hardware, lumber, and paint stores. It used its knowledge that such distributors wanted to improve their sales reps' selling skills to provide them with two-day courses on selling wood protection products to retailers. By improving the sales effectiveness of its appointed wholesalers, the manufacturer was able to gain access for its new line in over two thousand U.S. store locations. The training for the wholesaler reps was provided by the manufacturer's own sales personnel, who showed the wholesaler reps how to get the retailers to consider carrying the entire family of wood preservatives and protection products for outdoor deck owners, instead of merely picking one or two of the best of the total line sold.

Toyota Motor Sales in the United States is using its sales force to train its 1,089 car dealers on how to operate a used car operation more successfully.[4] Because of Toyota's limited vehicle availability, Toyota prices have remained firm with customers often waiting for new cars and paying the full dealer list price. Negotiating with customers for used car trade-ins was not therefore a key skill needed by Toyota dealers to clinch sales. However, conditions have changed now that Toyota has added car production capacity and more new competitor nameplates are coming on stream in 1990. Competition for car buyers is more intense. It is now critical for Toyota dealers to negotiate trade-in deals on used cars in order to sell their new models. Given that this will occur, Toyota must use its sales force to act as advisors to its dealers, in order to help them become not only skilled buyers, but also skilled sellers of *used* cars.

PPG Industries—Fibreglass Reinforcement Products Division

When Frank Green, vice-president of PPG's Fibreglass Reinforcement Products division, studied how to transform the division into a more customer-driven (instead of production-driven) company, he took a close look at PPG's approach to its distributors. He found that relations with PPG's sales reps and distributors were sporadic and that discussions about distributor sales versus forecasted potential were either informal, unreliable, or nonexistent. Given the critical importance of successful distributor partnerships with PPG to the division's overall health, he decided to launch a new course of action. He set in motion a training and planning program to turn his sales force into "consultants" to PPG's distributor "partners." Reps were asked to spend much more time overall and per call with the most important distributors and cut back the many, frequent, short calls to smaller distributors. The reps were asked to formalize their reviews with distributors, keying in on specific sales objec-tives for the distributors and asking them to indicate the specific supports they needed from PPG to help them accom-plish sales or market coverage objectives. After a year, this more formal, planned, and helpful relationship boosted both distributor sales and PPG's market and profit performance. Sales forecasts flowing back to PPG's factories were more reliable and were received with more lead time for schedul-ing, allowing for more cost-effective production and reduced inventories at both PPG *and* its distributors. Reps became proficient at making time for their key distributors and became more than order takers with these "partners." The reps became business advisors working hand in hand with distributors to fashion sales "work plans" with target quo-tas, exchanges of market information, and more tailored just-in-time distributor supports.

The five key roles of manufacturers' sales forces relevant to distributors or wholesalers are illustrated and summa-rized in Figure 3-4. Each of these roles is important in its own right, but of increasing importance are the roles of teacher, working partner, and reviewer. In the performance of these three roles, the sales rep from a manufacturer can become a true business advisor to its distributors. A recent poll of distributors indicated that they are very concerned about their reps making the transition to selling more tech-nical products. Clearly a manufacturer can greatly assist in such training.

As the sales forces of manufacturers become more skilled in providing strong guidance to distributors, they can enhance their value to the manufacturer. They provide more input into who should be appointed distributors in the first place (or who should be dropped) as well as providing

Figure 3-4. Factory salesperson's roles, tasks, and key skills.

Salesperson's Role	Tasks of Sales Reps for Each Role	Key Skills of Sales Reps by Role
"Teacher"	of selling skills, ROI selling of product applications knowledge of market knowledge of display techniques (walk-in business)	Excellent presenter, listener, counsellor, coach
"Reviewer"	of sales by product mix of sales vs. forecasted quota of competitive activity in distributor's area of inventory stocking vs. targets of distributor's participation in promotions	Analyzer, prober, trader of information, forecaster
"Working partner"	in joint "buddy calls" at end-user accounts in sales blitzes at targeted industries in trade show activity at shared booths in lead program follow-up, on demo day, distributor showroom programs	Hands-on demonstrator, leader by showing sales professionalism
"Ambassador"	in context of terms of sale, credit, warranties, leasing in context of promotions, contests, new product launches in context of co-op plans or advertising in context of ordering policies, assortments in context of pricing schedules, margins	Motivational selling-in of programs
"Ombudsman"	for distributor complaints on product performance for distributor credit, accounts receivable problems for distributor dissatisfaction about deliveries, back orders for distributor problems on order mix-ups, policies on assortments, minimums, nonstandard products	Negotiator, conciliator, empathetic confidante to distributor

feedback to their employers on what types of marketing programs will most closely match the needs and desires of such distributors. Cooper Tire has excellent relations with its dealers because its sales reps are tuned in to the dealers' financial and operational concerns.

Selling to Retailers

As retailers change, the sales reps of manufacturers selling to them must adapt. Blurred classes of trade require manufacturer sales forces to sell their products to nontraditional retailers. For instance, Xerox is beginning to sell typewriters and two small personal computers via Sears, a new type of channel with which its salespeople have no prior experience. Learning to sell to a new emerging channel can be very rewarding if it develops and becomes strong. Wholesale Clubs, for instance, did some $14 billion in business by 1988. Two companies that mastered the art of selling to this new channel have prospered spectacularly. Advanced Marketing Services Inc. of San Diego sold $153 million in books to Wholesale Clubs, and Jan Bell Marketing Inc., of Fort Lauderdale, Florida sold $120 million worth of jewelry to wholesale clubs, which account for 80 percent of its sales. If wholesale clubs total sales grow to $20 billion by 1990 as expected, Jan Bell will do even better because it is the primary jewelry supplier to this retail trade class in the United States.

Reps must customize their sales programs to retailers, whose store sizes and price positioning vary considerably. A manufacturer of stationary supplies must, through its reps, offer displays, planograms, deals, and co-op advertising that varies between discount stores, full-service department stores, warehouse clubs, drugstores, and bookstores.

As retailers grow in power, the manufacturer must often sell to such powerful customers with a team that includes salespeople, marketers, and customer service/logistics people, all of whom have special expertise in the program offered to the retailer.

The marketers on the team can discuss advertising and

promotion plans that they will make available for their brands. The sales rep team member can discuss possible display configurations, planograms, cross merchandising, and shelf visibility/location ideas. The customer service team member can discuss deliveries, returned goods issues, special labelling required, and other logistical matters such as invoicing, terms of sale, and expediting services.

Clearly, as retailers grow in power and sophistication, they are assessing more than just what products to buy, based on dollar sales potential. They are also assessing the manufacturer's track record as a supplier, its total retail program, and the return on investment (ROI) its products will provide for the retail shelf space devoted to the brands. This ROI calculation is a complex amalgam of gross margins and allowances calculated as a percentage of the space, inventory investments, and handling costs associated with the goods. Unless the manufacturer's sales *team* can get on the same wavelength as the retailer relative to that retailer's ROI formula as well as its preferred positioning for the product category, the manufacturer will never secure retail listings for its own lines.[5]

As some retailers' size increases, manufacturers are increasing their corporate acquisitions to grow their importance to the chains. As an example, Waterford, the $150 million manufacturer of cut crystal, bought Wedgewood in 1987 in order to sell $50 million in fine bone china to its same crystal accounts.

Sales Personnel Inside Retailer Companies

As retailers position and reposition themselves, they look for more professionalism among salespeople on the store floor, for those product categories where they feel salespeople are critical. Many believe this is the only way to differentiate themselves from low-priced rival retailers who offer little or no sales help to customers. Nordstroms offers extensive training to its sales personnel to teach them how to sell clothing to women. Ethan Allen also trains its "home decorating consultants," who sell its store home furnishings to couples shopping for furniture.

Not all retailers believe that more training and more knowledgeable floor sales personnel are always necessary for every product group carried. In fact, in some instances in-store customers prefer self-service or minimal sales assistance.

Consider for example, a department store. It is likely to sell as many greeting cards or men's shirts without sales help as with it, because people don't want (or need) assistance in picking out a greeting card, or a shirt by size and color. In other departments, the store offers only minimal service because customers want no more than this. For example, in departments that sell fine china, draperies, or wallpaper, the customer may want to ask the salesperson about available colors or patterns but then will wish to browse or study available patterns in a quiet place alone. Ikea, the Swedish furniture giant, leaves its shoppers to shop "in peace" by minimizing the use of floor sales staff. Its customers not only serve themselves, they provide self-transport, self-wrapping, and self-assembly of their own purchases. Any part-time sales staff who are "on the floor" are usually helping to stock and wear yellow shirts emblazoned with the words "Temporary help—Please don't ask me any hard questions."

Full-service salespeople are utilized in other departments, at a department store such as Sears, to sell "high-ticket" items such as home appliances, computers, carpets, or products sold as systems, such as home entertainment centers. This makes sense because the customer's concerns about product features, warranties, delivery, and machine operation require answers from knowledgeable salespeople.

For items where sales expertise is important to satisfy customers, retailers are screening potential candidates more carefully before hiring and then they are investing in continuous training programs (often using self-study courses, videotapes, or programmable videotext systems) to upgrade sales personnel skills. Developing retail selling skills, when the shopper of today has more store choices and demands high quality and fair prices, is a real challenge. Studies of excellent retail salespeople show that such people are very proficient at personalizing the benefits of what they sell to each shopper and at suggesting related items that could be used along with the primary purchases. These salespeople are skilled at using open-ended questions to probe for shoppers' real needs (instead of just asking, "Can I help you?" and getting a "NO, I'm just looking."). Retailers are also coping with the challenge of reducing chronic retail salesperson turnover by improving pay levels and building in compensation bonuses tied to higher sales achievement, to improve the total earnings capacity of top salespeople. Without attention to turnover, all the training and recruitment investments by retailers are a huge waste of time, effort, and money.

Summary

Middlemen are changing rapidly. Wholesalers and distributors are growing in scale and sophistication and becoming heavily committed to value-added services or specialty niches. Retailers are radically altering the product mix they offer and the formats that they use to sell such products. Department stores, for example, are shifting into the aggressive sale of services and are transforming departments into specialized boutiques—little stores within a big store.

As a result, manufacturers who sell to these middlemen are adapting. In addition, the sales personnel inside these retail or wholesale organizations are learning new skills.

For their part, manufacturers selling to wholesalers are teaching their reps to be *"business advisors"* with their distribution. Where they sell to retailers, reps are learning to sell "total programs" (not just products) and are often making sales calls as a team comprised of sales reps, marketers, advertising staff, and customer service personnel.

For sales reps inside wholesalers, the challenge is to upgrade their education and learn new skills, so they can cope with the advanced selling their more sophisticated companies demand of them. Retail salespeople are likewise becoming more professional toward shoppers via training, as their companies seek to carve out retail positions based on the in-store product and sales expertise of floor personnel. Fast-growth retailers such as Nordstroms have accomplished this with outstanding results.

The bottom line is that the sales rep job skills of suppliers' sales forces and those of reseller organizations are being transformed at many levels, to cope with the evolving changes in the external environment.

Further Readings

Anderson, Arthur, and Co., on behalf of the Distribution Research and Education Foundation. "Facing The Forces of Change: Beyond Future Trends in Wholesale Distribution." Washington D.C., 1987.

Carter, R., J. Cory, and J. Hoover, eds. "Industry Outlook 1990–1995." *Chilton's Hardware Age* (September 1988), pp. 54–90. Retailers, wholesalers, and manufacturers of hardware items comment on the changing market's impacts on them.

Harper, Doug, and John Bonnanzio. "Value Added: Profit Maker or Breaker?" *Industrial Distribution* (February 1987), pp. 33–35 (esp. p. 35; see chart on various value-added services).

McCartney, Robert F. "Churning the Cellular Phone Channels." *Business Marketing* (June 1988) pp. 49–58. Details on how cellular phone dealers and distributors are battling for market share using value-added services.

Michman, Ronald. "Trends Affecting Industrial Distributors." *Industrial Marketing Management Journal* 9 (1980), pp. 213–216.

Parr, Jan. "Good Merchandise and a Square Deal." *Forbes* (July 13, 1987), pp. 416–417. A profile of how Cooper Tire keeps its dealers happy.

Price, Margaret. "Distributors: No Endangered Species." *Industry Week* (January 24, 1983), pp. 47–50.

Rowe, Thomas. "Furniture Rental: Extra Profit Opportunities Await in a Lively Market." *Geyers Office Dealer* (October 1987), pp. 26–27 (special features on value-added services, variety of authors/articles, pp. 26–31).

Yoon, Eunsang, and Gary L. Lilien. "Characteristics of the Industrial Distributors Innovation Activities—An Exploratory Study." *Journal of Product Innovation Management* 5 (1988), pp. 237–240 (especially p. 229, Exhibit 1, "Recent Trends in Industrial Distribution").

For articles on the changing retail scene see:

Hafner, K., D. Cook, G. Geipel, S. Troy, and P. Houston. "At Today's Supermarket, the Computer Is Doing It All." *Business Week* (August 11, 1986), pp. 63–64.

Johnson, Tracy. "Shopping Swedish-Style Comes to the U.S." *Fortune* (January 20, 1986), p. 63.

Miller, Norman. "The New Immigrants—Europeans Are Changing the Face of American Retailing." *Chain Store Age Executive* (February 1986), pp. 16–18.

"Presidential Perspectives." *Industrial Distribution* (January 1989), pp. 30–42. The views of America's top distributor associations.

Stern, Aimee. "Retailers Restructure." *Dun's Business Month* (February 1986), pp. 28–32.

Chapter 4

Technology's Impact on Selling

The U.S. business landscape is littered with the beached bones of those who failed to adapt in a timely manner. When it comes to information automation, there is only one choice: become part of the steamroller or become part of the road.

—Richard T. Brock
Chairman, Brock Controls, Inc.,
Atlanta, Georgia

We are in the midst of a radical new technological age, the age of electronics. This new age is revolutionizing all aspects of life as earlier technological ages have done.[1] The mechanical age gave us mass production factories and railroads after the industrial revolution. Electricity, when it was discovered, ushered in the electromechanical age, an era of radios, appliances, and office equipment such as electric typewriters. The chemical age followed, providing new materials, drugs, fertilizers, detergents, and chemicals.

Today the electronic age is upon us, ushered in by the early discovery of the transistor, and today given added impetus by the microchip.

In the early 1990s, the average American home will contain over 100 microprocessors. These will be housed in microwave ovens, televisions, refrigerators, washing machines, dishwashers, thermostats, alarm systems, air conditioners, audio and video equipment, and automobiles.

The Impact of the Microprocessor on the Sales Rep

It should come as no surprise that the electronic age is ushering in big changes in the way sales representatives perform their jobs. In fact, in a write-up by *Fortune* Magazine on the "top eight supergrowth markets" in the 1990s,[2] three of the top eight markets are for products having profound effects on field salespeople: *cellular telephones, facsimile machines,* and *laptop computers.* Three other electronic age spin-offs are also beginning to impact sales forces: electronic mail (or voice message) networks, electronic sales training, and on-line data base extractions.

There are several motivations for the rapid adoption of these new tools by salespeople. The first is the push by managements for enhanced productivity from sales efforts and costs. With sales and marketing accounting for anywhere from 15 to 35 percent of total corporate costs, a productivity improvement of even 10 percent puts another 1.5 percent to 3.5 percent on the bottom line as profit. The second motivation is the use that can be made of such tools to bolster better customer partnerships and therefore improve the quality of these critical relationships and boost sales.

Finally, there is the need to respond to heightened competition, by fielding the most professional and efficient sales reps possible. This requires that new tools be adopted and integrated into sales forces to avoid falling behind competitors. With product parity the case in so many mature industries, orders go to the most professional reps among all rivals. It is therefore vital that investments be made in new technologies to keep reps "state-of-the-art" in selling against tough competitors. The company's basic competitiveness may be at stake. This competitive element varies by industry. In the sale of office equipment, more computers in sales and marketing may be needed because sending sales leads to the field and then tracking follow-up on them is most efficiently handled this way. In selling financial services, computers or advanced communication tools allow telesalespeople to handle customer inquiries faster and therefore provide needed rapid response times.

In a fast-moving and trendy market such as women's fashion clothing, laptop computers allow the sales force to let retailers know exactly where their orders are in the production-delivery system.

Cellular Telephones

The primary benefit of a cellular telephone is the way it can save a sales rep time. That is why in the United States, Canada, and Europe, cellular phones were first adopted by personnel most concerned with more efficient personal time management.

The two earliest customer groups to adopt cellular telephones were real estate agents and building contractors. To real estate agents, time is money because they are often working on multiple house deals and constantly driving around showing houses, meeting prospective buyers, presenting offers to sellers, checking out potential new house listings, or talking with other sales agents about splitting commissions.

A real estate agent's car is his/her office. Being able to conduct business on the go, with a cellular telephone, allows such agents to make maximum productive use of travel time. In fact, it expands the total hours in which they can make deals, appointments, and follow-up leads, while either sitting in traffic or in transit between a buyer and seller.

Contractors who build houses or are engaged in sub-trades such as plumbing, electrical work, heating and air conditioning installations, often juggle multiple jobs in progress simultaneously. Coordinating such activities at several job sites and still hitting building deadlines is a supreme challenge. A cellular telephone allows such contractors to use their trucks as a communications headquarters to all those people they must contact to ensure that construction materials and laborers come together at the right times and places to allow for successful just-in-time job completion.

While these time-management benefits are readily apparent to real estate agents and contractors who have to juggle schedules and tasks constantly, sales forces of major companies are not nearly so discerning about the merits of cellular phones. Companies that employ sales reps tend to look at the costs of these phones with great concern because line charges are high and many companies are uncertain of productivity gains. They wonder whether having a cellular phone is really going to generate sufficient revenues in sales to justify the added expenses.

Such companies usually decide to test cellular phone use in the field and see for themselves whether there are real gains from what many consider a new "toy" for reps. Field testing reveals several things. First of all, the benefits of cellular phones depend on a half-dozen factors that vary greatly among different sales reps.

Appointment Selling or Not?

In markets where a rep needs an appointment with a customer in order to make a call, and where sales-call activities during a workday are highly variable or subject to unforeseen changes, a cellular phone becomes a very useful tool. The rep can rejuggle the day as necessary. But not all sales reps need appointments to make sales calls, nor does it matter to some customers if a rep is delayed on a call.

As an example, a rep selling products to car dealers, body shops, or automotive aftermarket specialists such as muffler installers usually doesn't need appointments; where sales calls are planned in advance, they are often not set for exact times but rather specific to sometime in the morning or afternoon. A rep selling in this industry can be as productive juggling his day by using a telephone on the customer's premises or using a pay phone while stopping for a coffee break. A cellular phone is however, extremely valuable to a sales rep selling computers who must demonstrate the product to customers with whom set appointments have been established to "trial hardware and software" for potential hands-on users. Such customers are often unforgiving of missed appointments regardless of reason, because the demonstrations can involve many employees of the company. A cellular phone allows a rep to explain possible delays and rejuggle appointments, which often becomes necessary for a variety of reasons (including traffic delays, weather contingencies, and sales demos at some accounts taking longer than anticipated).

Rural Territory, Urban Territory, or Mixed?

A sales rep can get maximum use from a cellular telephone only if the cellular matrix broadcast area covers the majority of his or her physical territory. Otherwise, calls cannot be put through because of geographic gaps in cellular network coverage. Since most urban areas are well covered in a cellular grid, reps in such territories obtain excellent use of the phone. But not all reps have only urban territories. A rep covering four states may only be able to use the cellular phone in key cities, and not while in transit along highways in the wilds of Montana, the farmlands of Idaho, or wide stretches of Texas.

Many companies that have tested phones in both urban and rural zones have discovered firsthand that the benefits of such phones differ widely between such territories. This will become less of an issue over time as cellular network grid gaps become less apparent, but for now it is still problematic.

Customer Needs for Urgent Access to the Rep

Some customers have a much greater need to access the sales rep who services their account than do others. For instance, it may not be vital for a cosmetics manufacturer's sales representative selling beauty aid products via wholesalers to drugstore chain accounts to be contacted constantly. The wholesaler is providing ongoing inventory service, and the retailer itself has its own sophisticated warehousing. The products may not be critical to the ultimate shopper, so that a stockout in the shopper's preferred brand simply results in a brand switch.

Contrast this type of selling with a manufacturer who sells a critical production line component directly to Ford, Chrysler, or General Motors for a car. Car companies operate on just-in-time inventory schedules with parts fed to the cars on the assembly line as needed—with minimum extra inventories on hand beyond specific daily production needs. The plants may operate seven days a week and two or three shifts per day. So General Motors may want access to the sales rep to be as open and easy as possible in the event that any emergencies or contingencies arise in the flow of products for production usage. A rep with a cellular phone provides such accounts with critical access. The rep can be in constant touch with large automotive customers who can "make or break" the rep's sales performance. The rep's cellular phone allows him to contact his own company's order processing people, inventory control personnel, warehousing or shipping departments, credit department, pricing department (in marketing), or technical personnel to ensure that any problems that General Motors asks him to solve are handled as quickly as feasible. The rep can get the headquarter's team in his company to solve shipping problems, delivery mishaps, product defect issues, or pricing or invoicing errors. General Motors is therefore dealing with one central, knowledgeable contact that can be accessed constantly, rather than having to call the supplier and be passed around to multiple functions or be told that the person on the order desk is just filling in for someone who is sick that day. A cellular phone often allows a sales rep handling an important account to provide more credible customer service than that account could obtain dealing with the bureaucracy at the rep's own head office.

Direct Sale vs. Indirect Sale

Many manufacturers sell their lines via distributors, dealers, manufacturers' agents, or other forms of resellers. And many middleman companies have equipped their reps with cellular telephones because the distribution business is an intensely service-oriented undertaking. Distributors sell thousands of products to hundreds of accounts and their reps often need cellular phones to ensure that order turnaround, delivery completeness, and customer questions are handled expeditiously. If all of this is not done well, the distributor soon finds the end-user account switching to another distributor who can offer such services efficiently.

A manufacturer selling through distributors whose reps are equipped with cellular phones will service the distributor better if its own reps also have cellular phones. The communication loop at the field sales level is then more complete. The distributor rep and the manufacturer's salesperson can be in easy contact with each other, exchanging information that helps each of them keep the ultimate end-using account satisfied.

Traffic and Cellular Phones

In many large cities, traffic congestion and delays are a way of life. New York, Los Angeles, London, and Toronto traffic can be plagued by backups, road construction, detours, and the limited capacity of many streets and freeways. In fact, the highest concentration of cellular phones in the world is in Britain, in large part because of London's massive traffic tie-ups and the high costs of parking. A sales rep making six or eight calls in a day spends a lot of time not only stalled in traffic jams, but also looking for a place to park reasonably close to the customer's location. A cellular phone is a productive tool when such reps are stuck in traffic time delays beyond their control. The phone can be used to inform customers of possible appointment delays; the rep can also call his branch office to get updates on all sorts of news, from customer messages requiring follow-up to how his month-end sales results compare to forecasted performance. Useless traffic tie-up time can therefore become useful work time by means of a cellular telephone.

Laptops and the Sales Rep

Much has been written about how computer systems can confer competitive advantages to corporations. Information technology has provided competitive advantage to service businesses such as Merrill Lynch, American Airlines, and Reuters, as well as manufacturers of everything from apparel

(Haggar Co.) to window coverings (Hunter Douglas U.S.A.). In most instances, the computer is used to provide better linkages with customers either at the front of the value-adding chain, or with key vendors at the raw material supply end of the value-adding chain. American Airlines' Sabre reservation system is an example of a key customer linkage with travel agents and the public. Information, electronically exchanged, often permits more just-in-time purchasing or selling decisions. For instance, Hunter Douglas has used the computer to improve its logistics system so that it can deliver window-covering components to its two hundred nationwide fabricators of window coverings in days instead of the industry's normally slow time of two weeks. Faster information tied to state-of-the-art logistics has helped Hunter Douglas move its market share in miniblinds from 11 percent in 1982 to 43 percent in 1988.

Sales rep use of laptop computers in the very front end of the value-adding chain is only just beginning to gain momentum. In 1987 only about 15 percent of sales forces used personal computers (either desktop or laptop models), and forecasts by Info Corp. of San Jose. California, are that 28 percent of the sales force will be actively using personal computers by 1991, with the majority favoring laptop portables.[3]

What is becoming apparent is that the equipping of sales forces with laptops has reached the "jumping-off" stage for more rapid adoption in the future. Laptop visibility is higher, so that reps can see them more in the field and get to know who has acquired them. Figure 4-1 shows by stages how this process has been progressing. Adoption has begun to really gain momentum for three reasons. First, prices for units have fallen, so that units are affordable to more corporations. Second, the price-performance equation has also improved in terms of laptop quality. Units are lighter, graphic displays are better, batteries last longer, and memory storage with hard disks is now available. Third, the early adopters have been lauding the sales productivity gains possible with laptops. Usually a good "war story" of how a laptop computer helped a rep make a big-time sale is a better boost to laptop adoption than are cold productivity

Figure 4-1. Laptop computer adoption curve.

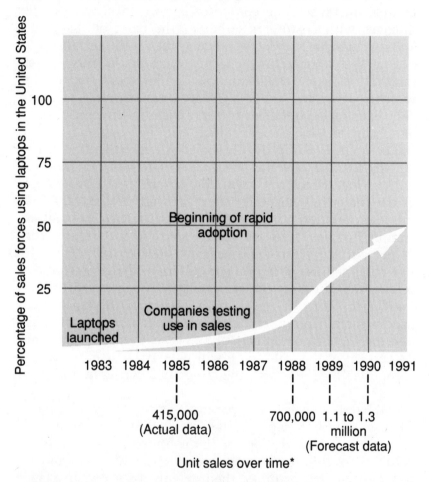

*Data originally contained in a more comprehensive article: Sue Gelford, "The Laptop Market Is Busting Out of Its Diapers," *Business Week*, November 14, 1988, p. 121.

statistics. Laptop field testing by companies is widespread in the sale of many different types of products, from insurance to agricultural, retail, industrial, pharmaceutical, and high-tech products. Sales productivity gains are crucial because the cost per sales call now tops $250 in many industries. Typically, after positive field testing of units has gone forward, companies decide to allow the balance of their sales reps to order laptops. For example, Ciba Geigy tested units over a full year and then decided to equip all its U.S. sales force (about nine hundred) with units, because positive field trials were documented and convincing.

Aside from making laptops more readable and expanding their machine memories, the industry has created a proliferation of software to make laptops truly user friendly. As one executive stated, "They're no longer considered toys, but real computers."

How Do Laptops Help Sales Reps?

There are several ways that laptops help reps and have proved successful:

- Improvements in *customer contact time*, made possible by more rep efficiency, provide big productivity gains. Reps can cut paperwork time and thus have more time for face-to-face calls. Gains in customer contact time have ranged from 15 percent at companies such as DuPont to gains of over 25 percent at Allegheny Beverage. At Eaton Corp., the Michigan truck components maker, laptops in the first full year of operation increased the number of rep calls by 24 percent.

- The use of laptops has also helped reps perform with more credibility and polish in front of their customers. Reps are better prepared to provide timely answers on the status of orders and shipments, which they access on their laptop. In addition, they can tailor calls because they are up to date on the account's buying history and product applications. These applications could pertain to either distributor or end-user accounts. In 1987 Kodak eliminated over 5.6 million pages of paper and over $1 million in costs by outfitting its reps with portable personal computers that give on-line accessibility to account sales histories, as well as order and shipment information. One of Kodak's largest savings areas is attributable to reps accessing computer data with their laptops *80 percent* of the time during nonworking hours (before work or after the workday ends). Laptops also assist reps in knowing inventory levels. They can then sell available stock for immediate shipment instead of selling products already on back order or scheduled for production too late to help the customer.

• A third advantage of laptop use has been that it provides reps with more professional sales presentations (through graphics packages) or faster turnaround in written sales proposals. Shell Chemical's sales force uses the laptop's graphic capabilities to make much more impressive presentations to customers. Some insurance agents have reported major gains in commissions because the laptop gave them the ability to quote, on a tailored basis, insurance needs of customers and compare such quotes to what customers are already paying to competitors.

With laptops, reps can compare features of the company's own offerings with those of its competitors, a feature that greatly impresses customers. Many sales reps discover that customers tend to believe that a computer doesn't lie. An analysis of a competitor's offer versus their own on a computer screen has great credibility with customers.

Laptop software can help standardize sales proposal writing so that a rep can produce a sales proposal much faster on a laptop than manually. For instance, in selling insurance, a rep can often write four or five sales proposal variations in a half hour while face to face with clients, because the basic proposal layout is already formatted and the rep merely types in specifics pertinent to each part of the software menu.

• Laptops are also used to help sales reps prepare both their call reports and expense reports with preformatted software. These reports can then be sent to the sales manager either electronically or via diskette. Sales reps are also quicker to use laptops when sales managers *mandate* the electronic filing of certain reports. At Shell Chemical, automating expense reports via laptops has greatly speeded up rep expense reimbursement, and is proving very popular with salespeople.

• Sales reps also use laptops to prepare sales forecasts for their accounts and territories, a very time-consuming task when performed manually. Spread sheet programs available for laptops cut this tedious chore down to size and allow a rep to perform as many forecast simulations as needed to produce a satisfactory result.

Other Major Laptop Sales Benefits

Equipping reps with laptops enables sales and marketing managers to roll out promotions more quickly, because rep questions about promotion details can be answered much more quickly through electronic mail, which can be linked to laptops. DuPont cut the time to launch a promotion in the Remington Arm's division from *two weeks to two days* because of the laptop system in place with its reps. Passing leads to reps electronically allows faster and more thorough lead follow-up and lead result reporting. In fact, replacing any bulky sales reports normally sent by mail to reps is possible with laptop-modem data transmission. When Owens Corning Fibreglas of Toledo equipped reps with laptops, it estimated that it sent twenty pounds less paper each month *to reps* as hard-copy reports.

Using laptops for communicating with reps is very critical in businesses that send reps all over the country in different time zones. Chevron Chemical recognized this laptop advantage and eliminated slow and cumbersome communication with its reps via phone, telex, and mail. Hewlett Packard cut the time its sales reps were in meetings from 13 percent to 7 percent (almost a 50 percent improvement) by equipping its reps with laptops for improved communications. But enhanced head-office to field transmissions are but one of many communication benefits provided by laptops. Reps who can communicate *with each other* using laptops can share awareness of new successful product applications. Order-closing time in some industries is also shortened when laptops are used for communications. This is because it takes longer to win orders when information has to be mailed back and forth between both head office and the field, as well as the field and customers, about engineered drawings, product specifications, written performance contracts, and price agreements. For companies such as Armstrong World Industries, laptops provide rapid cost estimates to contractor customers, on-site, a highly valued customer service in the time-urgent business of construction.

These many added benefits add up to one thing for reps—heightened professionalism with customers. Reps with laptops are more knowledgeable about accounts, more in touch with fellow reps and marketers, and more able to respond to customer questions, needs for quotes, needs for competitive comparisons, and needs for rapid order turnaround. Customers get the rapid yet thorough treatment they so highly value. And reps enhance their productivity by cutting wasted nonsales activities. It's a win-win equation.

Why All Sales Forces Don't Use Laptops

Despite growing evidence of their proven sales productivity benefits, laptops are still not in use in 85 percent of all companies. In some cases sales managements have not been able to convince senior management to part with the money. At several thousand dollars per sales rep, costs are a major inhibitor to the universal adoption of laptops. A company that believes in cost-justifying such purchases will be much more cautious in adopting laptops without ironclad guaranteed dollar savings. And cost-justifying laptops without, at the very least, a major field-test investment of them is probably impossible. This presents a catch-22 situation—there won't be adoption without proven benefits, but limited adoption is required to prove the benefits.

Adoption of laptops has also been slowed because the automation of any function, especially one as varied and subject to unpredictability as selling, is complex. Complexity may scare sales managers who are uncomfortable with changes the new technology will bring about in their sales forces. Since some changes are almost impossible to predict in advance, a sales manager who is already skeptical about computers will be disturbed to find out that laptop usage and applications often proceed in unpredictable ways. Even companies that do adopt laptops often phase them in over three years. Merck & Co., the drug manufacturer, is taking three years to outfit its entire sales force and learn applications.

Another reason laptop usage is not universal, aside from doubts about cost justification and application unpredictability, is that many sales reps, lacking keyboarding skills, may be fearful of computers. Pragmatically these reps believe that the time it takes them to learn the computer and become proficient at typing only takes away from valuable face-to-face customer contact time, harming their ability to make their sales quotas. Their own slower learning curve makes them leery of adopting laptops. Sales managers unskilled in computer use themselves are often leery of laptops as well, because they are afraid of training reps in an area where they, themselves, are not competent. Some managers also believe that more gadgetry in the hands of reps merely gets in the way of smooth sales calls and can build rep dependence on machinery for a good call at the expense of good old-fashioned sales "smarts." One leading management consultant says that such reps can become "scope dopes" and he decries laptops, refusing to acknowledge that such computers are any sort of key to truly effective salesmanship.

Laptop adoption will be very slow in any company that doesn't recognize that the driving force of sales reps is to meet or exceed forecasted sales goals. Providing laptops to reps either because marketing wants more market research or because management wants to cut clerical administrative costs, ignores the selfish benefits the reps find worthwhile. In fact, if reps have laptops pushed on them for reasons not important to their individual performances, a backlash may occur. If sales managers give laptops to reps with the expectation of big productivity gains, reps are almost certain to react negatively, feeling pressured to produce more, while at the same time coping with new work methods and foreign technology.

Smaller firms suffer no financial disadvantage in equipping their sales reps with laptops, because the cost per head is similar to the large company's cost. However, because they are very lean in terms of money and manpower, smaller companies are slower to adopt because they lack either the back-up staff to train the sales force during laptop launch or the cash flow from which to carry laptop costs.

A Final Word on Laptop Adoption

Despite the built-in inhibitions already discussed, laptop adoption is increasing. The reason is simple. As more companies adopt, those who don't will be left behind by competitors who have more "artillery" in the field. The laptop will become commonplace for the same reason the telephone and briefcase, sample book and product catalog are commonplace sales tools—its price-performance equation for the rep will be too powerful in most cases *not to adopt.* Selling and servicing time with customers can be enhanced with laptops in so many ways that within a short time a sales rep without a laptop will be considered out of touch, like the engineer who uses a slide rule or drafting board when the world has moved to advanced function calculators and CAD-CAM workstations. In addition, the price of electronically based equipment only goes in one direction—down. A laptop computer over time will therefore become more and more a bargain given its built-in capabilities. Failure to invest in laptops will one day be seen by sales reps as a lack of faith in them and their learning capabilities.

Fax Machines and the Sales Organization

Facsimile machines are becoming as pervasive as the office copier, and the words "Fax it to me" as commonplace a customer expression as "Give me a call." Figure 4-2 shows the rapid growth in fax shipments made to industry since 1985. In 1985, fifteen manufacturers sold fax machines. Today, thirty-five companies compete in this booming market. The one-millionth fax machine was sold in 1988, and Reliable Corporation, a direct-mail distributor of office products, predicts this total will climb to three million in 1992.

Sales reps and managers are opting for fax use because their customers are sold on it. However, facsimile transmis-

Figure 4-2. Fax purchases: total yearly (actual and estimated) in the United States.

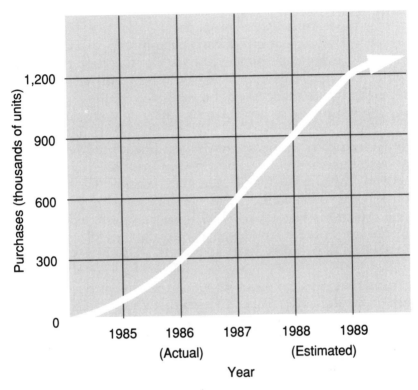

Data originally contained in a more comprehensive article: Jeff Rothfeder, "MCI Makes Move on the Fax Market," *Business Week*, November 21, 1988, p. 108D.

sion also offers a number of pivotal advantages to sales personnel. Fax saves on mail delays when reps must send documents to customers. In situations where reps sell to distant customers across multiple time zones, a fax message is far more efficient than even a personal call because fax machines operate twenty-four hours a day, remaining ready to receive materials even where time differences prevent the sender and receiver from actual telephone contact.

Aside from a fax machine's efficiency as an "electronic courier" when combined with a cellular phone, a sales rep using a portable fax machine can communicate with customers and his boss or peers by both voice and data links. In

California, real estate salespeople use fax machines in their cars to obtain copies of the latest real estate listings. By cellular phone, they then arrange appointments for their clients to see "just listed" properties.

A sales force equipped with portable fax machines can easily receive lead information to pursue new prospects while making sales call swings through the part of their territory where the lead originated.

New public-pay fax machines are beginning to appear at airports, in hotel lobbies, car rental agencies, convention and trade show centers, and major office buildings. These allow a busy, traveling sales rep to insert a credit card, wait seconds for approval, and then fax messages or documents back home to head office or ahead to customers. These units will eventually become as ubiquitous as automated banking machines. Some estimates of the availability of such units in the United States forecast that the number will climb above 20,000 by 1992. Wide availability of such pay fax units means that reps can send important documents to customers or headquarters right away rather than having to wait for overnight mail or courier service. Given the already large amount of time reps must spend in airports, hotels, and trade show convention centers as part of their jobs, such technology will greatly assist them in using hitherto idle waiting time to communicate important paperwork.

Electronic Mail and Voice Messaging

AT&T has determined that 75 percent of all business communications are not completed on the first try. "Telephone tag" is as much a national pastime as baseball and jogging. Electronic mail systems allow a sales rep to send or receive messages electronically via a computer terminal. The advent of electronic mail allows for much faster order processing when a company's distributors are directly connected to its factories. For instance, Shachihata U.S.A., a major manufacturer of high-quality, pre-inked custom stamps, used electronic mail to its dealers and cut order delivery times (compared to regular mail) from four and a half weeks to less than two weeks. Such systems save on memo writing and telephone tag, two wasteful activities with high costs. For instance, in a twenty-five-person organization, in which three memos per week per person can be avoided (at five dollars to nine dollars to type, copy, and distribute each memo by mail), $11,250 can be saved annually using electronic mail.

Voice mail, another technology, allows a rep to dial a system and, after entering a password, create or receive voice messages. A voice message being sent can be forwarded by the system to multiple parties. The advantage of voice mail over computer electronic mail is that it is easier and faster to speak messages than type them. And because voice messages are in a sender's own voice, the message can reflect the tone and sense of urgency of the sender much better than an electronic mail message on a computer screen can. Voice mail will catch on much more quickly when industry standardization of features and comparable pricing is in place. Currently, great confusion between different vendor offerings exists. It is very hard to compare alternative voice mail systems between vendors such as Siemens, Mitel, IBM-Rolm, and Fujitsu-GTE.

Both electronic mail and voice messaging tend to produce shorter messages than do long-distance telephone conversations, because the messages are concise and less idle chitchat takes place than on the telephone. In one study, it was found that sales reps using voice messaging systems had messages lasting an average of one and a half minutes, while a control group who used the telephone had an average message length of four minutes. Since call costs are lower (due to less time required), the savings accrued by introducing voice mail to a sales force can add up very quickly.

Electronic Sales Training

New sales-training methods can yield huge payoffs for some sales organizations. If new methods speed up a rep's learning curve, faster sales result. And if the rep is in a tough market, such as selling life insurance, moving up the learning curve has a double benefit—the rep is successful earlier and, as a result, less prone to quit. Electronic sales training can be accomplished using two basic technologies. One is teleconferencing, in which a company trains new salespeople using video broadcasts instead of bringing them, at great expense, to a central meeting location. Videoconferencing, which uses live broadcasts, can assist reps in learning about new products, new customer successes, and new promotions about to be launched that reps must be briefed or trained about. Data Quest[4] reports that videoconferencing equipment expenditures were over $500 million in 1988, up from only $70 million eight years ago at the start of the decade. As company markets become more globalized, teleconferencing by satellite is becoming a real benefit to link overseas operations for key presentations.

The U.S. Air Force uses videoconferencing to teach over 4,500 students each year. Such videoconferencing is often faster and cheaper than assembling all reps in a central location for their training. DuPont, which spent over $100 million to fly staffers to meet with one another, cut its travel expenses by $5 million through the use of videoconferencing. In addition, experts who can provide instruction can be used even though they may be unable to appear "live," since their video comments can be broadcast as a part of any teleconference.

Interactive Video

A second type of electronic training uses interactive video technology—a combination of a computer, a videodisk player, and a video camera. These pieces of hardware can transform the computer into a face-to-face sales training tool as effective as a lecturer. Here's how it works: A video of a client customer, typical of a normal sales prospect, is shown on the computer screen to a new sales rep learning to sell. The sales rep uses a touch-screen to select his response to the video client's sales objections, and the computer records and stores the student rep's answers. At the same time, the rep video records himself verbally handling the video client's objections in the manner consistent with the touch screen anwer he had provided to the computer. The computer and video client are preprogrammed then to respond to the answers selected by the student, in certain ways that require the student to respond further to new video client concerns or queries. Using the touch-screen, the student selects his answers and videotapes himself verbally "performing" such replies. This sequence continues in a multitude of different iterations all dependent on back-and-forth exchanges.

At the end of a session, a rep has handled a number of preprogrammed tough "real world" concerns of the video client shown to him. The computer scores his replies and advises him on how he's doing. The student can play back his own videotaped verbal responses that have simulated the selected touch-screen answers he believes most realistic to satisfy the video client's objections. After practice and repetition, the student learns not only the best ways to handle various client concerns, but also how he would look and sound to a given client. When the student feels he has mastered the replies and has a good tape of himself simulating a real client-sales rep exchange, he can take the finished tape to his sales supervisor for review. Interactive video systems of this sort use branching program logic. The sales trainees' responses to the video client prompt certain objections from the video client, which in turn must be resolved via the touch-screen selection and live videotaped replies of the trainee. Such video exchanges, where the rep can replay his own taped replies and learn from them, brings great realism into video sales training.

More and more of these systems will be used because results of such training for some companies using them are outstanding. Massachusetts Mutual Life Insurance saw productivity in sales revenue from new reps rise 15 percent once it adopted interactive video training equipment. However, one very great inhibitor to mass usage of this sort of system is the cost of the units, which can exceed $16,000 for the disk player, computer, and videocamera combination. If a company decides it needs a large number of the training units, investments can be sizable. Massachusetts Mutual Life spent over $1.7 million for 125 such units.

On-Line Data Base Extractions

The existence of on-line data bases, which can be tapped for information on target customers, is a major breakthrough for sales forces. For many years, marketing departments had to rely on purchasing customer mailing lists, which were often out-of-date or less targeted by line of business, size of company, or geographic location than was ideal. These lists are used to prospect for sales leads through direct mailers.

The existence today of computer data bases, which can be precisely sorted by standard industrial classification (a company's line of business), zip code, number of employees, and other criteria, allows user companies to finally give reps higher-quality leads resulting from mailings. In addition to allowing more precise targeting, these data bases also eliminate mailings that miss the mark because lists purchased are out-of-date. Electronic data bases such as Trinet (part of Nexis, owned by Mead Data Central Inc.), up-to-the-minute in terms of accuracy on target companies, can produce labels or printed lists to use for mailings or sales-call blitzes on certain customers in selected cities.

These on-line data bases can further assist sales reps by providing detailed account profiles that can be used during sales presentations. For example, a rep who is presenting to a Fortune 500-size company can improve his credibility when he is able to quote plant sizes; locations; and sales, marketing, and product profiles for the company's diverse subsidiary operations. A presentation can be custom-tailored for any company using the detailed data available from these electronic data bases.

Summary

Ten year ago, sales forces were not ready for the adoption of information technology such as laptop computers, facsimile equipment, interactive video disks, and the like. Computer literacy was weak, costs for such equipment (where it was available) were high, and much of the hardware available was less than optimum for field sales applications.

Much of this has now changed. The sales reps of today need to be more knowledgeable in front of their accounts about the status of orders, inventory, or promotions as more competitors swarm around their accounts for orders. Reps are keen to be able to tailor price by account, *faster*. Going back and forth to head office electronically for price quotes allows deals to be accomplished more quickly. Reps are hungry for the solid qualified leads made possible by new data bases. Electronic hookups allow reps at Chevron Chemical to get leads that are only twenty-four hours old. Reps enjoy the polish and depth that modern technology adds to their presentations, because they can really do their homework on potential customer operations. Reps appreciate the ease with which paperwork can be completed, stored, and transmitted with new automated methods.

In short, the automation of the sales force is picking up steam.

The acid test of any sales force technology adoption always comes down to answering three key questions: Does the technology help reps improve their customer service so that customers benefit? Does it help reps manage the territory more skillfully? And does it improve their impressions on customers so that sales gains are boosted? If the answer to these three questions is yes, then sales force automation will become a way of life for today's reps.

Further Readings

Earl, M., D. Feeny, M. Lockett, and D. Runge. "Competition Advantage Through Information Technology: Eight Maxims for Senior Managers." *Multinational Business* 2 (1988), pp. 15–16.

Eisenhart, Tom. "Automating the Last Frontier." *Business Marketing* (May 1989), pp. 41–46.

Gold, Jordan. "Breadth of a Salesman." *Computer Decisions* (October 7, 1986), pp. 48–57.

Goldstein, Mak. "Sales Force Salvation—Portables Make a Difference." *Sales and Marketing Management* (October 1986) p. 69.

Horn, Stacy, ed. *Conference Board's Management Briefing In Marketing*, 3, 3 (June–July 1988), p. 2. For a profile of Kodak's use of personal portable computers in its sales organization.

Housel, Thomas. "Video Teleconferencing—A New Training Tool." *Sloan Management Review* (Fall 1985), pp. 60–61.

Moriarty, Rowland T., and Gordon S. Swartz. "Automation to Boost Sales and Marketing." *Harvard Business Review* (January–February 1989), pp. 100–108.

Moskal, Brian S. "Distribution: the Last Frontier." *Industry Week* (August 1, 1988), pp. 63–68. For an in-depth version of logistics improvements made possible by information technology.

Taylor, Thayer. "How the Best Sales Forces Use Personal Computers and Laptops." *Sales and Marketing Management* (April 1988), pp. 64–74.

Taylor, Thayer C. "Laptops and the Sales Force: New Stars." *Sales and Marketing Management* (April 1987), pp. 50–55.

Urbanski, Al. "Electronic Training May Be in Your Future." *Sales and Marketing Management* (March 1988), pp. 46, 48.

Postscript

What All This External Change Means for the Selling Profession

Everything eventually deteriorates into hard work.

—Peter F. Drucker,
Author, professor, consultant,
and "father" of modern "management"

Sales representatives, because they interact with smarter, more sophisticated and demanding customers, distributors, and competitors, are transformed by the changes discussed in the first four chapters. When customers demand better service or improved quality they turn first to the sales rep handling their account. When distributors have complaints about deliveries or sales terms, the sales rep in their territory feels the heat the soonest, not the warehouse or credit manager back in head office. When competitors get smarter and tougher and begin to add value in ways that give a company "fits," the sales rep is always the lightning rod that sticks out in the competitive storm and gets hit by these competitive bolts of lightning.

The effective sales force responds to the challenge of change by learning new ways to sell, organize, and manage its accounts and to integrate into its way of life new tools that can help it change for the better.

Chapters 1 through 4 have cataloged some of the mega-

Figure P-1. The sales profession: the world of the rep.

The Way It Was	*The Way It Is Becoming*

Old Tools of Reps

• Car. • Briefcase. • Sample kit. • Literature. • Account book. • Computer printouts of sales results.	• All the old tools. • Laptop computer. • Cellular car phone. • Portable fax machine. • Electronic mail hookup for online sales results, order status, account profiles, and call reports.

Selling Skills

• Product knowledge. • Application knowledge at user level. • Time and territory management skills. • Dress for success. • Selling skills: listening, objection handling, order closing.	• All the old skills. • Business "advisor" to distribution. • Rep as a "territory manager." • "Solutions" selling. • Selling to upper management, executive-level selling.

Organization Forms

• Territory rep. • Product specialist. • Market application specialist.	• All the old ways. • Team selling. • Key national account specialists. • Vertical industry specialists. • Telesales specialists.

Training Methods and Emphases

• On-the-job with manager doing the coaching. • In classroom, with a sales trainer. • Additional courses: self-study, night school. • Company-"dominated" course content.	• More self-managed (as management ranks have been thinned). • Continuous lifelong learning concept, much more of it with outside courses (non-company) or self-taught via interactive video systems.

- Stop-start courses at specific times in reps' development.

- More teleconferencing training.

Prospecting and Presentation

- Cold calls or leads generated from mailings of purchased lists.
- Proposals typed and collated for account presentation.

- Leads from mailers using computer data base extracts of accounts up-to-date.
- Multiple on-line proposals presented using interactive software on laptops. Data base extracts allow for reps to stay up-to-date on account profiles and also competitor profiles.

---

changes that are creating new priorities and practices in selling. All of these radical discontinuities demand that reps grow and adapt. This is not easy—fruit is always bitter before it ripens. Reps will therefore face difficulties learning new roles, skills, and reporting relationships. It has been said that "thinkers prepare the revolution and bandits carry it out." This is certainly true in business. Business leaders recognize that change is the very essence of business life and they plan for it. The first half of this book is an attempt to see the shape of things to come in selling. And some of what is occurring definitely represents change of revolutionary dimensions. But it is reps themselves who are the bandits of change—the ones who must step into this revolution with energy and courage. Innovation is always a gamble, but refusing to innovate is not an option.

On the matrix in Figure P-1, the old ways of selling are outlined, and beside them are summarized the new ways of selling that are beginning to emerge. Any organization can read these factors and determine for itself how far its own sales force has come in responding to new external forces.

Part II outlines how all of these new sales rep priorities and practices will affect sales managers, who are themselves being transformed by the front-line revolutionaries they manage.

PART II

Sales Management in the 1990s

Chapter 5

Assembling Teams of Reps and Keeping Them Sharp

Is the skill pool of your workforce relative to the future getting better than your competitors? What you need today is a world-class workforce.

—Tom Peters,
Author, consultant
Quoted in *Training Magazine*,
June 1989, in an interview with
editor Jack Gordon

Sales managers engage in eight central tasks in their search to develop a "world class" sales organization. These tasks have remained constant for many years. They can be thought of as a combination of people-management and process-management skills.

Managers begin by recruiting, screening, and hiring reps. Task 2 involves training reps and readying them for sales assignments. Task 3 requires the manager to deploy the rep to cover markets, accounts, and geographic territory. The remaining five managerial tasks relate to the field: supervision, measurement of rep results, performance feedback and evaluation, compensation and rep incentives, and promotion of reps into managerial jobs or higher-level sales responsibilities. Figure 5-1 shows this sales-management task model.

With more volatile crowded markets, smarter customers

Figure 5-1. The sales manager's eight key tasks.

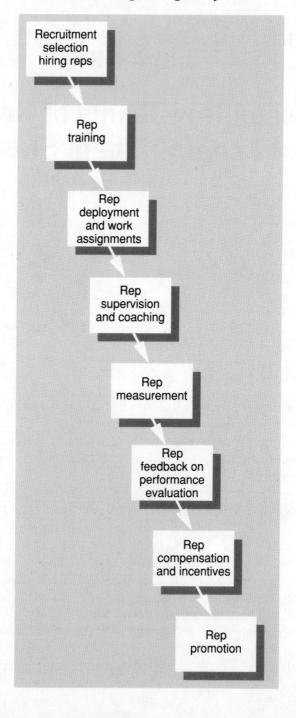

are demanding solutions, and with more consolidated sophisticated reseller companies, reps have changed. In the face of such changes, the model in Figure 5-1 must be updated. While reps are still recruited and hired, more of them are now college graduates, and more of them are women. Thus, selection of reps is more varied, with higher-level skills being sought. *Training* is no longer as operative a descripter of managerial actions as is *rep development*. As one astute manager once remarked, "You train animals, you develop people." Reps must be developed as specialists and as team players, since so much of selling is now a team effort. Deployment of reps to territories or accounts is today more complex, since some accounts are handled by telesales personnel, some by national account reps, and other accounts by rep teams composed of market, product, or applications specialists all working in concert. The sales manager learns to be a *network manager*, astute at team building and deployment as well as individual account or territory assignments. Learning International, a Stamford, Connecticut, training company, in a national survey of 3,200 managers, discovered that the number one measure of a sales manager's effectiveness today is his or her ability to orchestrate complex sales by bringing together a sales team.[1]

Supervision and coaching are altered more in degree than in kind. Reps still value and need individual coaching to handle problems with customers. But managers are more than ever leading *by teaching* rather than supervising task execution. The manager is becoming a teacher of self-managed professionals.

Measurement systems are an area of perhaps the greatest change because the old model shown in Figure 5-1 depended on measurement of an individual rep's results to drive both pay plans and performance appraisals. Today, with so much team selling, or mixed sales methods, more varied measurement schemes are needed. Assigning credit for sales is more problematic and complex in team selling. And new forms of sales specialization, such as national account management, often require a whole new set of sales result measurements. Telesales people and national account managers cannot be measured the same way as territory reps or product specialists can.

Rep evaluations and provision of feedback by managers remains a vital task. While reps should become self-managed, someone needs to help them accomplish this transition. Managers are the key people here. Their feedback can help reps analyze their sales successes and failures and set their own account goals; and the managers can provide advice about how the reps may want to go about achieving these self-imposed objectives.

The compensation-incentive and career-promotion task sets are more complex. Specialized selling or team selling calls for more creativity in rep rewards, because rep assignments differ so much from one another. In addition, keeping reps challenged is more difficult because many companies have fewer management positions into which the reps can be advanced. Forced by competitive dilemmas to become "lean and mean," many companies have thinned management ranks and flattened their organizations. There are fewer "chiefs to Indians" out there. The reps' needs for intrinsic rewards for achievement (as opposed to extrinsic pay or bonuses) demand that sales managers motivate the reps differently, with special work assignments, dual career-path ladders, and emphasis on "pride of profession" within the sales ranks.

Figure 5-2 is more representative of today's developing task set for sales managers.

The balance of this chapter focuses on the first three priorities: team building and assembly, sales rep development, and deployment of specialist sales forces.

Recruitment: The $2 Million Decision

Sales reps are one of the most expensive resources in any business. In fact, a rep who is hired by and stays with a company eventually will cost it in excess of $2 million. A good sales rep's salary can be substantial. As the saying goes, "Donkeys are cheap, but nobody ever won the Kentucky

Figure 5-2. The new sales manager's task-set priorities.

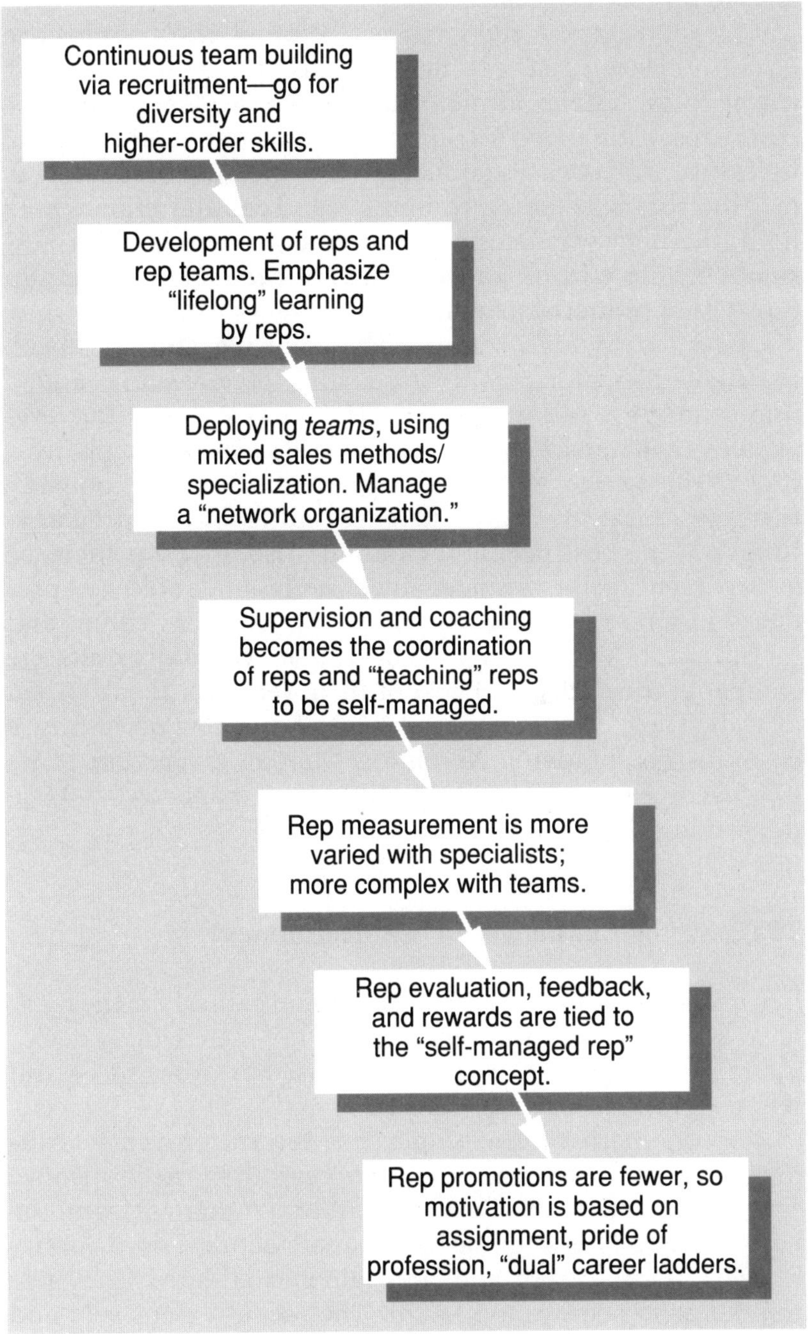

Continuous team building via recruitment—go for diversity and higher-order skills.

Development of reps and rep teams. Emphasize "lifelong" learning by reps.

Deploying *teams*, using mixed sales methods/ specialization. Manage a "network organization."

Supervision and coaching becomes the coordination of reps and "teaching" reps to be self-managed.

Rep measurement is more varied with specialists; more complex with teams.

Rep evaluation, feedback, and rewards are tied to the "self-managed rep" concept.

Rep promotions are fewer, so motivation is based on assignment, pride of profession, "dual" career ladders.

Derby riding on one." So managers who want good performers should hire the best.

In addition to a rep's salary, the other costs of reps are
large and growing. These include costs of an automobile, air
travel costs, hotel and meal costs, customer entertainment
costs, costs for a rep's training, samples and selling aids,
literature, and occasional incentive or meeting costs. And as
new tools such as laptop computers and cellular phones take
hold, the high wage costs typically associated with professional selling will be joined by *higher capital costs* to equip
reps with productive technology.

Given such high selling costs, spotting and recruiting
the right talent for a company's sales force assumes added
importance for sales managers. Higher costs raise the level
of sales that must be generated to still earn the company a
profit. Hiring the wrong mix of talent costs the company
two ways. First, its competitiveness suffers, by fielding anything but the best people it can find. Also, its costs increase
as a percentage of revenue, since the less-talented rep produces less revenue, but costs as much to train, equip, and
recruit as does a good rep. If this talent eventually quits the
company, the additional cost of turnover must be absorbed
as well. Thus, errors in recruitment often show up in future
costs to the company. Xerox loses about 15 percent of its
reps each year, a costly situation because it spends $100,000
per rep in salary and training annually.

The New Key Challenges in Rep Recruitment

Because sales managers invest in human capital for the long-
term benefit of their sales teams, they are increasingly deciding to hire on the basis of principles used by other successful
team organizations who recruit.

Sports teams, for example, use several proven recruitment principles to assemble a successful sports franchise.
They *continually* recruit high-caliber graduates from the
best schools. They emphasize balance, depth, and diversity
in their plans to spot and sign talented athletes. They pay
top dollar to acquire top talent. They scout extensively and

keep detailed charts on an athlete's performance, not only on average but in varied game situations.

They sell the athlete on *joining their organization* rather than yielding to the attraction of money or a signing bonus. They look for personality characteristics that will blend with those of the other members of the team and mesh with the objectives, beliefs, and values of their organization. They screen candidates with multiple interviews to get many different key opinions of the recruit before finally deciding on an offer.

Sales managers need to recruit continuously, rather than scramble each time turnover occurs or market growth opportunities present themselves and added staff is therefore needed. That means encouraging the personnel department to engage in continuous recruiting of possible rep candidates from a variety of sources, and then vetting these résumés through the sales managers.

The sales manager needs to establish stringent hiring standards for sales reps. For instance, college graduates represent a higher caliber of rep with more intellectual capacity and long-term learning potential than do lesser-educated rep recruits. Mark Twain is quoted to have said that "training is everything—a cauliflower is nothing but a cabbage with a college education."

The better educated rep has knowledge, which may or may not be exactly germane to the sales rep position. However, the intellectual horsepower of a more educated rep recruit proves that the rep has learned *how to learn*. In the long run, a front-line sales rep who knows how to continually reeducate him or herself will be best equipped to adapt to changing markets and customer needs.

In addition, with so many industries emphasizing the need for reps to become market or industry specialists, a higher-level college degree may be an absolute prerequisite to do well. For instance, Air Products Corporation sells 150 specialty gases of a very technical nature to very technically oriented customers, usually engineers. A rep must learn the right gas for the customer's application and teach customers how to handle these gases safely and for optimum results. It is far easier for Air Products to teach trained chemical engineers how to sell nitrogen, argon, oxygen, hydrogen, or helium than it is to teach them to be chemical engineers. In addition, because sales reps in Air Products find new applications for existing products or potential needs for new products, they provide key inputs for product research and design. Their higher education helps them greatly in this role, which goes beyond straight selling. Thus, in many industries, a college education is becoming a must for sales reps. A 1988 Dartnell survey of rep hiring in American industry showed only 59 percent of reps in 1977 had a college education. This had grown to 82 percent by 1987 and is still increasing.

Screening Reps for Personality Attributes and Attitudes

While education is becoming a more vital criterion for selling, sizing up prospective reps for desired attitudes remains essential. Unique traits and qualities in reps are demanded of different types of sales specialties.

For instance, industrial reps who sell to trade accounts such as dealers or distributors have to be comfortable in cementing long-term relationships and taking responsibility for managing regular low-level contacts with a great deal of independence and self-sufficiency. A rep doing consultative selling of big-ticket products or services (such as computers, telephone systems, consulting services) requires a strong team orientation, an academic bent, status and image consciousness, and the ability to interact comfortably with top executives. So consultative sales reps, in order to succeed, require personalities very different from those of relationship sales reps who work through dealers.

Reps who sell on commission in a retail environment or via cold calls on different prospects every day need another set of personal traits. These include very high physical energy levels, strong money motivations, a competitive mindset (which makes them indifferent to customer rejection) and extroverted personalities (they really enjoy people).

Shelby Carter, former senior vice-president of Field Selling Operations at Xerox, used to seek out five traits among rep candidates, which he believed would lead to sales success at Xerox selling equipment. He sought out people who were:

- Tough but pliable—committed to success
- Action-oriented (decisive)
- Incisive, able to think things through
- Balanced—work is not their whole life
- Solution- instead of problem-oriented

So any sales manager hiring reps should think through what rep traits are most essential in terms of the market changes taking place in his or her business.

Balance in the Rep Team

A sales team needs to be balanced, with some reps older and very experienced and others young and eager to learn. Veterans on any team provide stability, maturity, and seasoned guidance to younger team members, who bring fresh enthusiasm, energy, new ideas, and a desire to compete and impress older teammates. A sales manager may want to blend the skills and personalities of the young with the existing, more experienced reps.

Balance is also important in rep skills and backgrounds. It is often a good idea to blend together people of varying backgrounds and life experiences. Sales problems tackled by the team then have some guarantee of being approached from quite different perspectives.

Depth by Position

Sports teams always recruit with the eventual goal of replacing older players and having back-ups at each key position. In a sales context, this means that when a sales manager is looking for new people, he or she should sort out where that recruit will fit in down the road. Will the recruit be able to

back up, a vital skill now scarce in the sales team—perhaps
only evident in one or two reps? Will the new rep make a
good replacement for someone retiring shortly? How quickly
could the new rep adapt to fill in for a key veteran who gets
sick, is transferred, has an accident, or in some way has to
be replaced?

Diversity in Experience Levels and Gender

Not all reps recruited come directly from school—many,
having worked in other fields, take up selling. Sometimes, in
the recruiting search for reps, a manager should look for
work experience that will provide the rep with a unique
affinity with his or her customers.

For instance, Apple Computer often hires ex-teachers to
sell its computers to school boards, teachers, and administrators. The reps uniquely understand the education field
from the inside and can appreciate the pressures and concerns of professional teachers and educators. One of Lear
Jets' top salespeople is an avid pilot himself, having served
as a navy pilot and trainer of other navy pilots. Past work
experience can provide candidates with valuable customer
synergy-building experiences, while ensuring that the new
recruit will probably have fun in the sales role. When a
manager knows from recruiting that a rep will find the
selling job itself enjoyable, quite apart from financial rewards, chances are excellent that the rep will be a valuable
catch.

Sales managers are beginning to wake up to the fact
that the other 50 percent of the population, women, make
terrific sales reps. Women are the leading sales performers
in many businesses, including real estate, computer equipment, health care products, pharmaceuticals, data processing services, and consumer packaged goods. Women are also
making a mark in the sale of high-ticket medical equipment,
financial services, and telecommunications products.[2] Although only 15 percent of all sales reps in the United States
are women, the figure is growing rapidly. According to Na-
omi Rosan, a leading sales recruitment executive, "Women

have a high energy level and are perceptive and effective communicators. They seem to be able to focus on selling solutions and don't have the aggressive old boy attitude that some salesmen have developed over the years."[3]

In an era of selling total service solutions to customers, women reps' skills in listening and gauging customer needs (where they frequently outperform male colleagues) are all the more valuable.

Gail DeWitt was Philips Medical Systems North America Inc.'s top sales rep in 1987, a year in which she sold $10.8 million worth of medical scanning equipment to U.S. hospitals. She attributes her success to both issues covered in this section—experience relevant to customers and superior listening skills. First, she was an X-ray technician herself for many years before becoming a sales rep and selling to X-ray department customers in hospitals. Second, Gail uses her listening skills to sort out the key buying influences in hospitals where highly bureaucratic and politicized decision making takes place for the big-ticket capital purchases she sells (average sale price of $1.4 million per sale).

As Gail remarked, "The worst thing about salesmen is they talk too much." By listening, "you figure out what people want and find a way to give it to them. . . . It's like being a detective."[4]

Selling Prospective Reps on Your Company and Screening Them

Just as sports coaches sell top athletes on all the benefits of joining their organizations, sales managers should recruit top prospective sales reps, who are often recruited by many companies. Astute sales managers, having selected the top two or three candidates, should sell this short list of prospects on all the company's strengths, from its future growth prospects, new products or services to be launched, ethics, and concern for employees to its financial health, track record in community affairs and environmental and safety issues, and geographic scope and ambitions. Many of these are not of direct concern to the rep candidate in the job for which he or she has applied. However, in making final judgments about where to begin a career, a candidate does care deeply about the vitality and ongoing health of the company he or she is joining, its treatment of its employees, and its ongoing beliefs about its social and community responsibilities. And this is a two-way street. Sales managers need to take great pains to hire only those people who will fit into their company's culture. Sales reps have to buy into a set of shared values that will guide their actions in selling. If the manager believes the rep can live those kinds of values everyday, his or her chances of success are much higher.

In screening the final candidates, it is a good idea to get other senior management people who are not directly in the sales manager's line of business to interview them and make some judgments about their suitability. In this way the sales manager gets a second or third opinion from people not subject to the same sort of pressure to fill a vacant sales job and cover accounts currently not covered. There is always a great risk that sales managers will hire a rep based on the prospect's immediate abilities to bring in orders rather than his or her long-term potential. Because of this pressure for results, the sales manager may overly weight the importance of a candidate's past sales experience at the expense of other important prerequisites to long-run potential, such as education, integrity, and the ability to shoulder more responsibility in the future. In some companies, such as Digital Equipment, where team selling is often the norm, members of the sales team actually screen new rep candidates to determine whether they will fit in as team players.

Screening for "Team" Players

With sales managers orchestrating sales teams, an important criteria in hiring involves looking for prospective reps who are "team players." Operationally, this means that a sales manager needs to look for and test candidates for traits such as:

- Their ability to cooperate and encourage others with whom they will work
- Their willingness to share praise with fellow reps instead of seeking credit only for themselves
- Their willingness to trust others in sharing information and tasks when working toward a common goal, instead of being anxious about controlling all aspects in the selling process
- Their focus on problem solving for customers as the primary concern, instead of secondary issues such as how recognition or rewards will be apportioned later on if the sale is successful
- Their eagerness to learn, as opposed to attitudes that suggest they will see themselves as wiser or smarter than others on the sales team

The manager needs to seek out reps with confidence and integrity but without egos so big that they will simply never make good team players. If the manager suspects that the prospect needs to hog the limelight too much, is intolerant of others in matters of selling, or is unduly critical in attitudes to others, the manager should look elsewhere. Candidates for whom working independently is the primary attraction of sales, will not fit in an organization where coordinated teamwork is the key to sales results. Such candidates are better left to gravitate towards the more entrepreneurial, lone-wolf types of sales positions, such as selling stocks and bonds.

Team Selling As a Multifaceted Concept

Team selling by a company can take place in several different ways. At DuPont, team selling involves sales reps, technical staff, and manufacturing all making joint calls on customers. Teams are specializing in certain industries such as paper and pulp, and the company gives the team freedom to make decisions and manage its small sales team as a business. In this way salespeople are more heavily involved in working with DuPont's manufacturing personnel and assure customers that they get what they need, instead of what DuPont might want to make. In addition, when research and design personnel make calls along with DuPont's reps, the reps play a stronger role in product development.

A different concept of teamwork is used by IBM, which combines its reps in joint selling efforts with the sales staff of its value-added remarketers. IBM's value-added remarketers combine vertical application-specific software with IBM hardware to sell turnkey systems to small- or medium-size accounts. The team orientation of an IBM rep thus involves working more with dealers. This rep-reseller team effort is similar to what Caterpillar does in linking its sales reps with its eighty key U.S. dealers. They go in jointly and assist contractors (end-user customers) in a consultative selling process to ensure that the contractor gets the equipment needed to fulfill his or her project commitments. Sharp Electronics Corporation of America has gone from selling no national accounts to 250 in two years by teaming up with its equipment dealers. Dealers sell Sharp's entire line of fax machines, copiers, computers, and retail systems along with its own reps and are paid variable commissions based on their involvement in landing such contracts or servicing them.[5]

A third type of sales team consists of many reps from the same company, all skilled in different products, and targeting a huge account's complete product needs. This is the type of team selling General Electric did when it landed the General Motors Saturn Division contract for all of Saturn's electrical needs. By coordinating their efforts, a team of forty General Electric sales engineers sold Saturn on single sourcing hundreds of General Electric products. They escorted all the key General Motors "specifiers" on tours of General Electric's factories and exchanged specifications that met all General Motors' concerns from cost to delivery to quality. General Motors had solid input into the technical standards that General Electric would build into the products made for it. And for its part General Electric was open about exchanging traditionally secretive specifications data.

Team selling can clearly involve the sales group in coordinating diverse functions in a company to assist customers, in coordinating distributors or dealers' efforts in joint customer activities, or in coordinating multiple reps across diverse divisions to go after a major national account's total business. Figure 5-3 illustrates this concept.

Developing Sales Reps

Sales managers play key roles in the increasingly critical role of sales rep development. In companies that are small or medium in size, the managers *are* the trainers. In large companies where a full-time training staff is set up, the managers have input to shape new courses and a key role in seeing to it that reps obtain timely training. In addition, the sales manager can provide after-the-fact feedback to trainers about how much specific courses have improved the rep's abilities and results.

Increasingly, sales managers are involved in training because they themselves are also being reeducated in order to stay in touch with customer or competitor changes. While sales training methods have changed with new techniques such as interactive video programmed learning and expert systems, there are "big picture" shifts in training being overseen by managers.

Rep development programs are *more diverse* than ever. In an age of multiple specialization and team selling, reps must take many *more* courses than in the past. At Xerox, a world leader in training reps, sales personnel take much more training in system selling and total account management than was the case only a few years ago. The emphasis is on selling systems, not "stand-alone" boxes to customers. Bell Atlantic brings its very best 60 (of 250) reps into an intensive 13-week course (stretched over 9 months) to discuss and study how leading-edge technology can be offered to customers in solutions for their problems.

Examples of other new course priorities for sales forces, beyond system selling, key account sales, or high-tech solution selling, include teaching reps how to deal better with distributors, training reps to do total value-added selling,

Figure 5-3. Team selling: three variations.

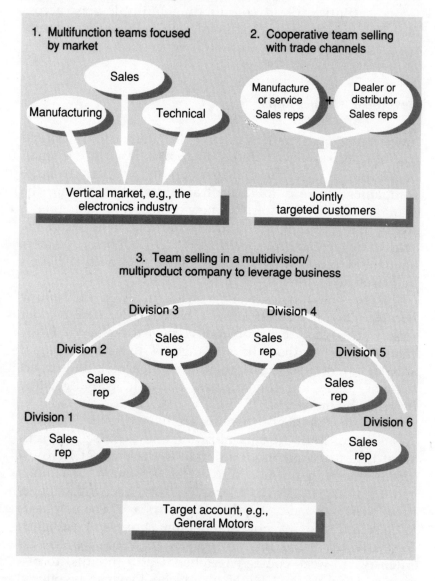

and training reps *as teams* to update their sales methods after extensive competitor analyses.

Cooper Tire is a company that teaches its reps how to get on the same wavelength with tire dealers and discuss problems dealers have in the dealers' own jargon. Reps can talk knowledgeably with dealers about return-on-inventory investment merchandising programs, displays, and co-op ad programs as well as orders, credit returns, and deliveries.

American Airlines now offers its reps a "quality work-shop," where reps learn how to sell the company's value-added services, such as its Sabre reservation system, instead of merely focusing on pricing.

Burlington Industries brings its sales force selling home furnishings into one-day sessions in which account handling teams analyze product by product how to beat the competition in each account. These sessions take place quarterly. To underline the importance of this new competitor-focused training, Burlington presents plaques to its three top-performing reps at these sessions.

Sales managers should be constantly thinking about what *new skills* their reps need to develop in order to become self-managed, confident performers. It is the job of the sales manager to push for *new* rep training courses, to ensure the rep's development is relevant to the changing pattern of competition and salesmanship required. Auto parts suppliers, in this vein, are putting their reps through training in the Japanese language and culture, to assist them in penetrating accounts such as Nissan, Toyota, Honda, and Subaru.

More Intensive Training

Another changing thrust in rep development is to immerse reps in *more* comprehensive training about their customer's industry. For instance, Merck, Sharp & Dohme, the pharmaceutical company, invests very intensely in training its pharmaceutical salespeople to be credible to both physicians and pharmacists. Merck trains its reps in the basics of medicine—anatomy, physiology, and diseases. Then it trains them in a six-month to one-year period on the properties of the products they will sell. Phase 3 involves a course on how the reps' products actually affect target diseases and outlines the medications' strengths and disadvantages. Part of phase 3 requires the rep to work in a hospital learning the practical aspects of a doctor or nurse's life on the ward, including seeing the effects on patients of different Merck medications.

After all this training, Merck reps receive periodic training updates in the field about developments in treating diseases specific to the drugs they sell as well as any new drug treatments emerging from basic research.

In an industrial/commercial context, IBM is teaching its reps to be experts in specific industries such as banking or retailing, to the point where 75 percent of IBM U.S. reps (whom IBM calls *marketing reps*) are specialized to some degree. IBM views as one of its greatest challenges training its sales staff to stay abreast of customer needs, even though these change daily and weekly. The thoroughness of a rep's training has to be gauged continuously.

Thorough and diverse rep development can differentiate a company's sales force from that of its competitors. For instance, nobody in the security business (stocks, bonds) trains its sales force as intensely, as often, or in more new ways than Merrill Lynch does. As a result, Merrill Lynch produces reps who can bring in sales in excess of $200,000 per year within a short time after starting in the securities industry. No competitor has this track record for sales productivity. This sales force manages to service over five million customers, and Merrill Lynch's profits top its industry every year.

Empowering Reps to Become Lifelong Learners

In an era of multiple specialists, sales teams, and more competition, sales managers need to establish a mind-set among their reps to "stay in touch" through continuous reeducation. The managers play a key role in teaching reps to study the industries or end users to whom they sell. They can teach reps how to put convincing, economically based sales proposals together that provide justifications to purchase the rep's products, as the rep moves up to sell to senior management decision makers. The sales manager can instruct reps in orchestrating the company's total skilled resources, so necessary to providing total customer satisfaction. Managers are encouraging reps to evaluate their skill strengths and weaknesses relative to their job needs. In this way the reps can take charge of identifying gaps in their training, rather than putting all the onus on the sales manager to suggest and develop their skills. The reps can also adapt and grow if they are in tune with their own strengths and weaknesses. Reps who constantly stay in touch by going to relevant courses are well positioned to take advantage of any career broadening prospects that come along, whether a promotion or a lateral transfer. In addition, training can be a real motivator to reps, a tangible investment and vote of confidence when the company relieves them from field duties periodically to send them on special courses. When this happens continuously, the rep realizes the company considers him/her a valuable resource regardless of how senior or experienced he/she happens to be.

Matching Manpower and Markets: Sales Rep Deployment

In the 1990s sales reps will need to be deployed in a much more analytic fashion, because of both the high costs of selling and the fact that a revenue increase of 10 percent in many industries often translates into a 30 or 40 percent gain in the bottom line. Clearly, deploying an expensive resource more scientifically can yield higher payoffs.

Sales managers must manage *more analytically* the two sides of the deployment equation, namely the selling mix to use and the market mix to aim at. Figure 5-4 illustrates how this rep deployment equation is changing and that sales managers can choose from many sales methods and need to constantly update targeted accounts and distribution channels.

The problem of making ideal selling mix decisions and

Figure 5-4. The sales rep deployment equation: the old way and the new way.

Rep configuration + Selected target markets = Rep deployment equation

Old way	• Rep configuration was usually standardized to one method of sale, i.e., face-to-face selling by territorially assigned reps.
	• Selected target markets were updated only periodically because account turbulence was low.
New way	• Rep configuration is complex with telesales reps, specialists, and team sales groups.
	• Target markets (end-consuming accounts, and channels of distribution) are volatile, in constant flux due to entrepreneurial economy and global competition.

staying abreast of market shifts for rapid deployment changes involves sales managers in quite separate types of analyses.

Defining the Ideal Selling Mix

Matching up manpower to markets is much more complex than it once was. For example, consider the case of a company selling original equipment and replacement parts to other industrial companies.[6] Until 1983 it was profitable and growing. When its growth slowed in mid 1983, it decided to take a closer look at its selling methods to determine if it was deploying its sales organization properly.

Its sales managers had traditionally relied on face-to-face selling, by its own territory reps, to all types of accounts. When the company analyzed its customers in detail, it discovered that its largest accounts were beginning to buy whole systems from single sources rather than assembling systems from different component vendors. Because the company's products were becoming more technically complex and because the company made a variety of components, suitable for systems selling, it recognized that its largest accounts required team selling by reps and technicians. It decided that it should formalize the team selling of systems, in a national account program.

Its small accounts, it discovered, had not been called on, in many cases, in more than two years. Face-to-face selling was not working well because the average order size was too small for its field force to bother with, yet many of these small accounts bought replacement parts that carried above-average margins. The company decided it could afford to contact all its small accounts at least once a month using telesales personnel.

It also decided to continue covering its middle-size accounts using field reps calling face-to-face.

As this case illustrates, sales executives today must evaluate different selling mix options on the basis of the option's cost, coverage efficiency, and fit to how the customers want to buy. It took more than three years for the company to work all the "bugs" out of its radically new selling mix because, as it organized to meet customer needs, it discovered that it had to develop separate ways to reward, measure, and coordinate the efforts of distinctly different sales methods. Now it is well on its way to considerably higher sales growth and profits as a result of a multifaceted selling approach.

Keeping Track of Account Changes

In order to sensibly match reps to account potentials, today's sales managers must rely on the computer. Software is available to assist in the redesign and rebalancing of sales rep territories that is required by rapid customer changes.

Manually redrawing the boundaries of sales territories is extremely time-consuming, often taking months. So even though the geographic center of buying activity may be shifting in cities and states, the task of redesigning sales territories has always been unappetizing.

New census bureau data will be coded by geographic coordinate in a level of detail that will allow mapping of market potentials for any area of the United States (not only the urban areas, which cover 60 percent of the population). When these data are used with software from private companies, sales managers will be able to create visual maps of territory potentials, within specific boundaries, and then quickly compute how changes in any boundary rebalances the potentials between them.[7]

Studies have shown that the use of new software to redesign territories, which better balances market potentials between reps, can boost sales anywhere from 2 to 7 percent.[8]

In addition to making greater use of computers for rebalancing territories, sales managers can use data bases to pull off lists of high-potential accounts according to line of business, size, number of employees, and specific zip code address. For example, if a sales manager of a printing products manufacturer wanted the names and addresses of all the top corporate executives in the printing industry in Chicago worth more than $1.5 million in sales, this kind of list could be sourced from a data base such as Dun and Bradstreet's Marketing Services Division (via Dialog Information Services, Palo Alto, California). The variety of other data base systems available on line are listed and described in "Online Access Guide" (from Online Access Publishing Group, Cicero, Illinois).

Account profiles and locations territory records must be constantly updated because they can become obsolete fairly quickly. To underscore this need, *Business Week* reported that in 1989 more than 18,500 small businesses in the United States were involved in mergers and acquisitions that would have resulted in company names and headquarters changing (for the merged company). This activity has steadily increased from 12,500 per year in 1985.[9] Building a good customer data base has another big advantage: The sales force can access the customer files in looking for cross-selling opportunities for additional products the company makes. It is far easier to sell a second or third product to an existing account than to acquire a whole new customer.

The Effect of Changing Distribution Channels on Deployment Decisions

Quite apart from the effect of shifting end customers and multiple selling options on deployment, there is a third factor complicating the manpower market matching equation.

Distribution channels are often more complex than they used to be.[10] Consider the example of a company selling personal computer software. As Figure 5-5 illustrates, up till the mid 1980s this company sold its software to three channels of distribution: computer stores (such as Computerland), data processing supply dealers, and original equipment manufacturers of computers.

After the mid 1980s, six additional distribution channels emerged: mail-order catalog supply houses, systems houses, wholesale clubs (such as the Price Club), office stationery dealers, specialized software retailers, and buying groups of retailers such as college campus bookstores.

Thus, when the sales manager in the software producing company undertakes deployment of his or her reps, entirely different skills must be trained into the reps who handle quite different channels.

Reps assigned to system houses need extensive technical skills and would perhaps be paired with technical back-up personnel.

Reps assigned to deal with original equipment manufacturers (OEMs) need key account handling skills, including advanced skills in negotiation, and logistics systems that provide OEMs with just-in-time ordering and delivery services.

Reps working through data processing supply dealers or office stationers require skills in designing dealer training and incentives to assist these dealers' sales personnel.

Reps selling through computer stores or software specialist retailers need to understand retailers' needs. Reps must excel in merchandising, display, and cooperative advertising program execution.

In the example cited, a sales manager would need to

Figure 5-5. The phenomenon of channel-choice proliferation.

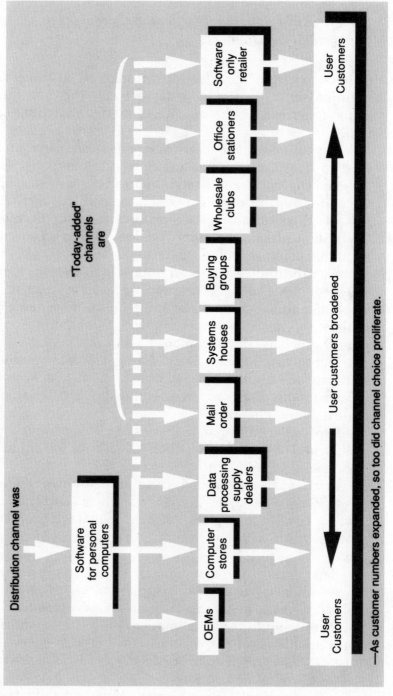

deploy reps to channels where they were most confident and competent.

Clearly the managers of sales organizations are learning to manage more complexity—in sales methods, data base usage for market updates, and skill matching—with increased channel variety.

To prepare themselves for this task, sales managers need to hone their planning and analysis skills. They can be helped by both computer courses and intensive workshops, where they can get together and learn how to make the trade-offs between sales coverage alternatives and evolving changes in buying profiles and preferences.

Summary

This chapter highlights how the first three major components of a sales manager's job will be altered in the 1990s—recruitment, rep development, and rep deployment.

Recruitment has shifted into the search for more diverse skills as new specialists are required and teamwork is essential. Screening reps for higher intellectual capacity and team cooperation is essential.

Rep development demands of managers more creativity and the ability to instill in reps a commitment to "lifelong learning." Deployment decisions require managers to target and retarget accounts more frequently based on shifting target customer potentials.

Managers then need to match this network of rep selling options to the different marketing channels and a volatile shifting customer base. This calls for heightened planning and computer analysis skills.

Further Readings

Ames, B. Charles, and James D. Hlavacek. *Market Driven Management*. Homewood, Ill.: Dow-Jones Irwin, 1989.

Cardoza, Richard N., and Shannon H. Shipp. "New Selling Methods Are Affecting Industrial Sales Management." *Business Horizons* (September–October 1987), pp. 23–28.

Cespedes, Frank V., Stephen X. Doyle, and Robert J. Freedman. "Teamwork for Today's Selling." *Harvard Business Review* (March–April 1989), Reprint No. 89205, pp. 1–8.

Magrath, Allan. "To Specialize or Not to Specialize." *Sales and Marketing Management* (June 1989), pp. 62–68.

O'Connell, William. "A 10-Year Report on Sales Force Productivity." *Sales and Marketing Management* (December 1988), pp. 33–38.

Shapiro, Benson, and John Wyman. "New Ways to Reach Your Customers." *Harvard Business Review* (July–August 1981), pp. 103–110.

Shook, Robert. *Ten Greatest Sales Persons*, New York: Harper & Row, 1978, pp. 82–84.

Sovner-Ribbler, Judith. "Which Database Solves Which Marketing Problem?" *Sales and Marketing Management* (July 1988), pp. 53–55.

Stevens, Howard. "Matching Sales Skills to Customer Needs." *Management Review* (June 1989), pp. 45–47.

Sutton, Howard. "Rethinking the Company's Selling and Distribution Channels." *Conference Board Report* No. 885 (1986), (especially page 3 on manufacturer's expectations of channel use in the early 1990s).

Webster Jr., Frederick E. *Field Sales Management.* New York: John Wiley & Sons, 1983 (especially p. 152 on models for rep call plans).

Chapter 6

Meaningful Coaching and Leadership of Sales Professionals

Effective coaching requires a balanced discussion in which the leader first tries to understand before he or she tries to be understood. . . . Great leaders are great partners first because they have learned to manage both human and business needs.

—Steven J. Stowell
Co-founder of Center for Management and
Organization Effectiveness,
Salt Lake City, Utah
June 1988

Peter Drucker has said that outstanding organizations only succeed when "common people achieve uncommon performance." This was never more true than for sales management. While it would be nice to believe that sales managers could groom all superstar sales reps, in fact most have a mix of performance levels on their sales team. Sales stars often overachieve regardless of coaching or compensation. But getting the average reps, who often comprise 60 percent of a typical sales force, to perform better makes the biggest difference in a team's overall results. To coax outstanding performance from the team, excellent sales managers learn to raise the performance "bar" so that their people have to stretch their talents to get over it. But they cannot raise the bar to such a height that the performance standard is well beyond the abilities of their people.

In Chapter 5, it became clear that the spotting and developing of talented reps can go a long way to ensure that the average proficiency level of a sales rep force improves each year. Combining this blend of reps with astute modern computer-based deployment tactics assures the company that market opportunity matching is optimum.

But coaching reps requires a great deal more than assembling a team and setting up customer assignments in an efficient, sensible fashion. If that is all any team needed to do to win, the teams with the most talent would always win, and certainly those that combined high talent with great game plans would dominate all other teams. In real life, of course, that is not the case. Teams with great game plans often lose. And teams stacked with talent often perform below par and are beaten by other rivals with less raw talent who are simply better motivated and coached.

In business, a great field coach in sales can be just as powerfully important to a company in defeating its competitors for market share, as a sports coach is in winning a championship pennant. Sports teams with long, outstanding records of winning invariably have superior coaching. And behind most outstandingly successful sales organizations are superior district and national managers, who know, as Steven Stowell eloquently put it, how to manage both human and business needs.

How Coaching Sales Reps Is Different Today

Given that field coaching reps is important, what is it about today's reps that creates unique challenges for their managers?

There are several factors that require managers to modify the proven coaching techniques that have been used for many years. First of all, sales reps of today are better educated. Not only do they begin selling with more college education, they are committed to lifelong learning and are therefore assimilating new skills all the time—from knowing more about computers to possibly taking night-school courses on psychology or negotiation to upgrade their interpersonal skills.

More educated reps are more independent in their judgments of situations and more knowledgeable about how to analyze selling situations, grasp new concepts, and try new sales techniques. In short, reps with higher education expect their managers to sell them on their ideas, not tell them what to do. Persuasion works, but ordering reps around does not. This phenomenon is, interestingly enough, also occurring in sports—where the older, more autocratic coaches ("it's my way or the highway") are all being replaced by more effective, younger coaches who can relate much more to the new players and sell them on their goals for the team, to gain players' personal commitments to excellence in practice and play.

Coaching today's reps is also being affected by the stress levels experienced by the sales force. Personal stress is heightened by dual-career marriages and reps trying to balance career needs and family pressures despite a job where travel and time away from a spouse or children is often unavoidable. The stress can be greatest when small children fall ill and must be cared for at home by one of the parents, or when entertaining important customers after hours at social functions interferes with family obligations. In a modern marriage, spouses tend not to tolerate a partner who does not hold up his or her end of the family-rearing responsibilities. And with many reps taking night-school courses to upgrade skills continuously, it isn't only travel that is interfering with the rep being a supportive spouse or parent.

On a professional level, pressures are greater because of two major forces at work—more competitors are present in accounts as businesses become globalized (many new rivals are out there whom reps never saw before!). Free-flowing information across the globe has dramatically reduced the time gaps in penetration rates between nations for new products. For instance, color television penetrated Europe far more slowly than it did the United States—by a few

years, but today compact disc players have penetrated
households at identical rates on both sides of the Atlantic.
The world is a global shopping plaza due to free-flowing
information. New products maintain their market edge for
less time than they did in the past. Copycat products make
their appearance in markets much sooner than they used to.
In the 1950s less than one-fourth of new products making
their appearance in the United States were duplicated by
rivals overseas within five years. Today more than two-thirds
of new products invented in the United States are matched
by foreign companies within the five-year "window."

Thus, sales reps whose products had an edge, lose it
faster. And as product performance parity occurs, the rep's
professionalism may be *the* major reason for the sale. This
puts more stress on reps than it used to, when the rep's
products had the competitors' products beaten hands-down
on performance.

The combination of more stress and more professional
education in today's reps adds to the challenge faced by
sales managers. Reps want more autonomy and shared decision making, but they are also in greater need of a coach
who is empathetic, fair, and compassionate about their
personal pressures. Managers need special skills and finesse
to handle these pressures.

The Pressures on Sales Managers

Sales managers, as coaches, also face new, somewhat different pressures in the 1990s. They must upgrade their own
training just as aggressively as reps must, which can put lots
of pressure on their own families as they take courses or are
trained away from home.

In an era of downsizing, many companies have thinned
the ranks of sales managers, thus widening the manager's
span of control. A manager will therefore have perhaps 33 to
50 percent more reps to supervise. For instance, a manager
might go from having eight reps to twelve reps reporting to
him/her. That means 33 to 50 percent more expense accounts
to sign, more salaries to review, more performance apprais-

als to give, and more rep training and incentive compensation plans to administer. It pulls the manager into more territories, often boosting his or her own travel time—and this increases stress as the typical frustrations of living on the road escalate (from late planes, to problem rental cars, headquarter communication hassles, and so forth). Because the manager with more reps to supervise tends to spend less time coaching each rep, there is pressure to do the highest-quality job communicating face-to-face in field coaching sessions. Quality supervision replaces closeness of supervision. The manager's own superiors are probably also putting pressure on him/her to boost productivity. *Sales and Marketing Management* magazine found that from 1978 to 1988, actual sales productivity in the United States did not keep pace with inflated selling costs in a wide variety of industries. Clearly, senior managements in such industries cannot allow that record to continue if they wish to remain competitive against global, intransigent competitors. This is especially the case in industrial selling, where personal selling is a far more important marketing tool than advertising is.

The sales manager is caught in this tug-of-war between senior management's goals for maximum output from the field, and the sales employee's interest in acting independently in the field, with autonomy and shared decision making. Successful sales coaches must always balance the need to *care* about their sales reps as people, with business pressures to *control* them, because they are costly resources. A sales manager perceived as caring only about business results and carrying out management dictates, winds up with employees who feel alienated and abandoned. They wonder how the manager will function if the business hits rough water. Will the manager help them grow and develop? Should they bet their futures on such a leader? This is how reps think when the sales manager works too hard for rep compliance and control at the expense of maximum output.

Should the sales manager be perceived by superiors as too people-oriented, they become anxious that he/she is too soft on subordinate reps and will "give away the store," not focused enough on ensuring that orders flow in and shipments flow out.

More than ever before, the sales manager of today has to learn to be both bottom-line committed and a fine coach and employee partner. Learning this takes courage and skill, and few sales managers get much help or sympathy from above. They could echo the words of Tommy Lasorda, the Los Angeles Dodgers manager, who said, "I found out that it's not good to talk about my troubles. Eighty percent of the people who hear them don't care and the other twenty percent are glad you're having them."[1]

Great Sales Force Coaching

Since coaching reps can be stressful and difficult, it is worthwhile to take a close look at what makes for a great coach, and what constitutes excellent coaching.

Successful field coaching of reps requires that sales managers recognize three preconditions. First of all, the manager must set aside the time to devote to coaching activities. Some experts believe that in a typical sales management position, 75 percent of the manager's time should be spent in the field coaching reps.[2] Second, to be truly effective, most coaching must be done individually with reps, in sessions that last anywhere from thirty-five to forty-five minutes, immediately prior to or following rep activities with customers. This allows the coaching advice to be relevant, timely, and credible. As such it will sink in and have impact. Coaching that is delayed or out of sync with applicable situations is not nearly so effective. Although a certain amount of coaching of sales reps in a group setting is possible, most coaching of reps should be tailored to the individual to reflect the operating realities of different reps, customer sets, and distributors in a territory.

Third, the benefits of coaching are not truly realized until a trusting relationship has been established between sales manager and rep. Because all coaching involves confronting mutual problems, unless trust is present the rep being coached may not feel the manager has earned the right to be as firm and direct as the situation requires. The manager's authority is not sufficient in itself to ensure that genuine coaching sessions will occur. In most meaningful coaching sessions, the sales manager shouldn't over dominate. Yet this frequently occurs in the absence of a trust partnership. Because trust involves a certain amount of shared values and experiences, developing a trusting relationship takes time. Sales managers must be realistic and recognize the time-consuming nature of trust building.

A great coach performs several key roles for sales reps. Each of these is illustrated in Figure 6-1. Sales managers provide quality instruction and teach reps specific skills needed to manage their territories and meet or exceed sales forecasts. Sales managers mentor reps by providing a variety of constructive supports for reps to perform at their best. Sales managers are pathfinders and standard bearers, leading reps into new markets, toward new goals, and then providing firm, clear communication and feedback to reps on how they are doing in their quests. Sales managers are problem solvers and rep protectors, assisting reps in tackling the inevitable problems that crop up in day-to-day selling, and protecting reps from unreasonable, unproductive demands made on their available selling time by marketing people or other administrative departments.

Let us look in turn at each of these in more detail.

The Instructor-Teacher Role

Sales managers should help reps integrate what they learned in their classroom training about products or selling skills with what experience is teaching them "in the street." In this regard a sales manager can provide quality instruction to reps, on the spot, in "curbside conferences" before or after sales calls about:

• How to correctly spot and probe for genuine customer needs.

• How to categorize customers by sales potential and in ways that make the rep smarter in qualifying business prospects *or* more able to quickly typify the key buying influences in an account. Customer categorization helps reps stay

Figure 6-1. Key coaching roles of field sales managers toward reps.

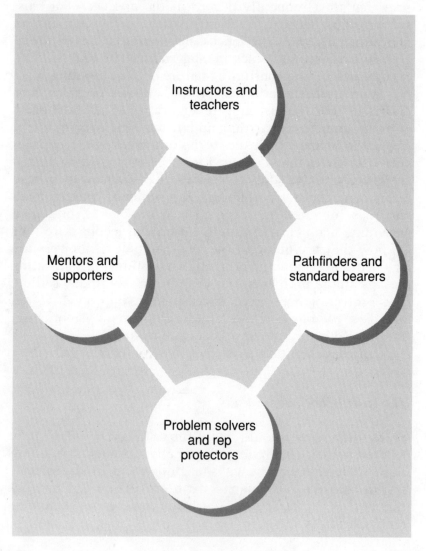

organized, because they can more readily use their accumulated knowledge of what works for customers, who are similarly categorized. Reps are far too busy to treat every customer in a unique way. They must learn to use categorization to mentally retrieve those selling skills that helped them win orders for customers whose buying processes are very similar. The reps can be coached "to organize their prior selling experiences into sales situation categories, and then to associate selling strategies."[3] Ciba Geigy has tailored different sales presentations on the same ethical drug to physicians, depending on how the physician has been categorized by volume usage, medical specialty, and type of clinical practice. Managers, because of their deep knowledge of markets and customers, are key catalysts in teaching reps to categorize accounts.

• How to study and categorize *competitors*. Competitors can usually be typified in four ways. *Passive* competitors are slow to react, because they either believe their market position is solid, or their "laid back mentality" results from disorganization or lack of resources (to do anything aggressive). Competitors may be *selective*, taking action against the company only in very specific and selective ways. For instance, a selective competitor might react if you attack its key accounts but not be provoked if you cut your prices.

A competitor may be labeled *aggressive* if it takes prompt and vigorous actions on many fronts—sometimes acting only on news that you are planning something (as opposed to an actual overt move by you in the market).

A competitor may also be classified as *unpredictable* if it is highly flexible and shapes itself to each market situation in different ways. Sales managers who teach reps to better understand competitors are providing them with information useful in setting and modifying sales goals in the midst of changing competition in the local territory. For instance, reps covering key urban territories are often subject to much more aggressive and numerous competitive maneuvers than are reps in larger, more rural territories, with smaller towns and cities to cover.

• How to optimally lay out routing plans for customer call cycles, depending on various accounts' sales volumes and territory. The manager can guide reps in defining the "A," "B," or "C" target accounts and then help the rep determine feasible call schedules for each, given their geographic location.

• Sales managers can provide quality instruction on sales calls, and what the rep can do to achieve desirable outcomes. Managers can be dispassionate about which approaches used during calls work best and/or how these can be fine-tuned to be more effective. This really improves a sales rep's *adaptive* selling skills. Often a manager accompanying a rep can see ways for the rep to better his or her handling of customer objections or to improve closing techniques for orders. Teaching reps self-assessment skills is a vital part of a coach's role.

The Mentor-Supporter Role

Great sales coaches ultimately want their reps to be self-managed high achievers, with the independence and confidence necessary to meet increasingly complex selling challenges.

To help reps reach this state of self-sufficiency, managers can be personally supportive in a number of ways. They can collaborate with reps in finding solutions to account problems (instead of being unwilling to assist because they're too busy). They can make sure reps get the resources they need to perform properly—whether this is formal training, sales tools, samples, literature, or new technology such as a cellular phone or a laptop personal computer. They can show genuine empathy for rep problems and obstacles—personal and professional. Indifference or neglect are surefire destroyers of rep trust. Managers can encourage reps with constructive criticism and expressions of thanks for the rep's contributions and value to the company. Managers should accept some personal responsibility along with the rep for solving selling difficulties instead of suggesting they are somehow "above" these issues. They can listen *actively* to their reps, avoiding a one-way communication style, so that reps can air feelings to lower the barriers to helpful two-way communication.

Managers can mentor reps with both task assignments and career moves. In most sales organizations, reps can progress to successively higher sales ranks, without necessarily being promoted into management. For example, an organization might have four rungs on the sales rep career ladder, each with different titles. A rep may begin as a sales representative and progress to an account representative, senior account specialist, and senior sales executive. Each of these different positions might require of the rep different levels of demonstrated sales experience, results, and education. A sales manager can mentor reps along this path as they qualify for each successive assignment based on experience, more training, and demonstrated track records of outstanding sales results. If a rep feels the manager is his or her biggest "booster," the rep is encouraged to make extra efforts and live up to the manager's high opinions of him/her. For instance, if a successful rep can progress more quickly in the sales ranks with a transfer to another division of the same company, and the manager *delights* in such programs, the rep will take great pride in being affiliated with such a selfless manager.

Reps can be mentored with one-time project assignments to develop or round out their talents. For instance, a rep could be assigned to be the resident expert about a specific new product or market application. The manager could ask the rep to train others at a national sales meeting about the product or to share his or her knowledge of the vertical market application. Asking reps to be teachers of other reps adds value to the rep's self-esteem. Of course, sales managers can also mentor "managerially" inclined reps by letting corporate senior executives know who such reps are and when these reps appear ready to step up and assume a supervisory job within the company.

At Merck, Sharp and Dohme, top sales people can aspire to a half-dozen career-path development assignments. These include stints as trainers in the field or head office, jobs in field communications or meeting services management, or more technical positions as health-education liaison people.

Any of these mentoring initiatives provide reps with challenge and creativity that helps them enjoy their work more. They gain intrinsic rewards from their job in addition to the usual extrinsic, monetary rewards for hitting sales targets. Special training assignments and teamwork task-force assignments for reps are also becoming more important motivators when companies have fewer promotional career opportunities due to restructuring. A change in responsibility in a current job is one of the few ways to keep people from "plateauing," becoming bored with a lack of job challenge.[4]

The Pathfinder-Standard Bearer Role

If all it took to be a leader were implementation and problem-solving skills, there would certainly be more leaders around. But one obligation of leaders is to communicate where they want their organization to go. As John Sculley, Apple Computer Inc.'s CEO, has said, having "a compelling vision of what you want to do" (with a company, a business, or a sales force) is the surest way to "inspire people around you to believe as fervently in the idea" as you do.[5]

Defining the sales force's primary purpose and goals keeps it on track. The vision acts as a magnet to focus effort and attention. Warren Bennis calls this "the management of meaning," convincing others to align themselves with your dreams of possible success. Great sales coaches need to be able to do this with the sales team as a whole and then to translate these umbrella goals, aspirations, and expectations into individual territory goals, which is situational leadership at its best. A sales force led by a vision is far better than one pushed by precedent and past success, which may not be sustainable in a volatile environment.

In the context of one-on-one rep coaching sessions, the manager's role consists of clarifying his or her expectations of the rep. Goals the manager wishes the rep to strive for have to be clear, firm, and explicit. Some goals are numerical, such as sales volume targets or other goals within such targets (such as new-product sales volume growth or new-account volume sales growth). Some goals and expectations are much more qualitative, such as the rep becoming more skilled and comfortable at making senior-executive-level sales presentations or handling customer complaints with more tact or efficiency. Nonetheless, regardless of what goals are set, any one-on-one coaching must involve being absolutely clear about expectations of the rep's performance.

Having set standards for the rep to strive for, the manager coach has to seek the rep's support of the vision, to gain commitment to the goals. The coach can only attain excellence among the reps through a shared vision commitment. In some ways, the manager is selling him or herself to the individual members of the sales team. The coach can then, during follow-up sessions, provide clear and honest feedback on how he/she sees the rep's progress against these standards. Together, rep and coach can explore the impact of different future actions on the attainment of the goals and put together action plans that emphasize solutions to any problems the rep is having. This is much more difficult to practice than to write about, because some reps who need the most coaching are often the *least interested in being coached*.

In addition, because managers are under enormous short-term time pressures for results, they often display their frustration and doubt in coaching sessions, causing reps to get defensive and feel attacked. Such sessions inevitably involve confronting problems in sales results head-on. Only those coaches who can learn to be supportive and caring while still being clear and direct about goals can accomplish this. The manager must also be supportive when things are clearly not going well for the sales rep. If the manager dwells on the negatives too much, the rep feels devalued and demeaned and likely emerges not very optimistic about his or her chances of making the necessary changes to get sales results back on track. When managers demonstrate their positive support of employees to overcome obstacles and pull out of any slump, they build not only more confident reps but more motivated, committed long-term employees.

The Problem Solver—Rep Protector Role

Sales managers also function as problem solvers and protectors for reps.

Because sales managers have a vast exposure to customer problems across multiple industries, cities, and over a longer time frame, they can be of terrific assistance in helping reps in the field to troubleshoot customer problems. The manager may have seen a particular customer problem surface dozens of times, where it is a unique event to the rep solving it for the first time. In addition, the manager usually has a larger network of contacts to talk to and get input from to help solve customer problems. These contacts can be leveraged to get speedier action on behalf of a rep who may feel somewhat isolated in the field. For instance, the manager may be able to provide just-in-time assistance to a rep who is trying to get an expedited shipment or credit approval on a "held" order. The manager's intervention can also resolve internal company conflicts to everyone's satisfaction. In addition, the manager can provide advice to reps on complex product-selection decisions where neither rep nor customer is quite sure which product specification would be best in a "tricky" application. Sales managers can always ask their peer sales managers for advice to help a rep, something a rep is usually not comfortable doing directly.

In the 1990s, voice mail will speed up communication and can assist field managers in helping reps troubleshoot customer problems. These systems cut down on "telephone tag" and allow individuals to network their communications efficiently. This is very critical in situations where troubleshooting involves a large-volume customer who is being handled by a team of reps (or a team comprised of multiple functions such as sales, the lab, manufacturing, customer service, and marketing personnel). Voice mail systems allow a manager to send one message to all reps, without having to resort to calling each separately, and from the manager's tone of voice reps can immediately determine how urgent the message is.

As a protector of reps, the field manager has to keep

them liberated from all but the most critical paperwork, meetings, controls, and reports. Paperwork, as one sage observer has described it, is "the cholesterol of any organization clogging the arteries" of companies who can ill afford it.[6]

Asking reps to second as market research data collectors, invoice collectors, or business prospectors (when direct mail is more efficient) is simply cutting into their available face-to-face selling time. Paperwork and meeting minimization is the responsibility of sales managers, who must support their reps in their primary role—selling products and developing accounts to the fullest.

An excellent coach in sports must often "speak up" for the players with club executives who foster distractions that interfere with their play. These include booking them for public appearances, autograph signings, media questions, and so forth. Sale reps are no different. Frequently, marketers, customer service people, inventory ordering people, credit people, and so on are interested in asking reps to take on tasks or fill in forms irrelevant to sales generation and of no direct personal benefit to the rep.

As chief protectors of their reps, managers need to deregulate such activities and vociferously fight the bureaucracy's cramping effects on sales time. It is amazing how many reports, meetings, controls, rituals, and forests of paper seem vital, until they are removed by the manager who is stressing the *rep's point of view*.

Jane Lee, a rep at Apple Computer, described her sales culture's deregulation of wasteful activities as *"short on red tape, long on trust."* It is the manager's task to see to it that reps' face-to-face sales time is kept at an absolute maximum and not bled away bit by bit by well-meaning but external demands.

Summary

The speed of the leader always determines the rate of the pack, particularly in sales management, because the results of any leadership lag always show up early—in poor sales force morale, sales results "off forecast," eventual loss of market position, and ultimately high staff turnover. This chapter has emphasized the vital role of coaching in managing today's sales professional—a more stressed, but better educated caliber of rep. The need for *quality* rep supervision has never been greater, because field managers have more persons reporting to them and close supervision is quite impossible. Sales managers must coach the best from their reps by understanding what constitutes coaching excellence.

The coach is an instructor, mentor, pathfinder, problem solver, and protector for reps. And coaching is a process of compressed, timely advice that has to take place in intensive sessions in the field, where the sales action is occurring. Not all sales managers are equally adept at all their roles. But a savvy manager who can master most of these roles can become a great coach, meeting both the revenue needs of the business and the personal and development aspirations of reps themselves.

Further Readings

Alexander, John W. "Sharing the Vision." *Business Horizons* (May–June 1989), pp. 56–59.

Bennis, Warren. *Why Leaders Can't Lead.* San Francisco: Jossey Bass, 1989.

Everett, M. "Who Needs District Sales Managers?" *Sales and Marketing Management* (December 1989), pp. 54, 56.

Feldman, Diane. "Helpful Hints for Salespeople." *Management Review* (June 1989), pp. 9–10. About helping plateaued salespeople by using challenging assignments.

Ford, N., and O. Walker, Jr. "Differences in Attractiveness of Alternative Rewards Among Industrial Salespeople." *Marketing Science Institute*, Report No. 81-107 (1981).

The Successful Strategist. Alexander-Norton Newsletter. (July–August 1988).

Verespej, A. "Stress! Stress! More Stress!" *Industry Week* (June 1989), p. 19.

Chapter 7

Redesigning Measurements and Rewards to Fit the Sales Force of the 1990s

The more dependent the work of an organization is on the work of its professional knowledge workers . . . , the more the organization must attend to their getting the professional and personal satisfactions that keep them inspired and in place.

—Theodore Levitt
Editor, *Harvard Business Review*
Quoted in "Management and Knowledge,"
Harvard Business Review, May–June 1989 (page 8)

If there is one area that taxes both the creative and analytical abilities of sales managers, it is designing a performance measurement-reward system that stays current with changing market objectives and shifting sales force specialization. When one considers the different kinds of reps an organization employs, it is reasonable to conclude that compensation plans based on a "one size fits all" philosophy are bound to fail. A single compensation plan for all fails to recognize key differences between a national account rep, a telesales rep, and a territory rep. Each rep probably emphasizes different product mixes to suit customers, and each sells to accounts with different buying cycles. Measuring results against one sales quota formula would therefore be folly.

Measurement systems that aren't given a fresh look inevitably lose relevance over time, because companies may shift emphasis from selling individual products to total customer solutions. Alternately, they may utilize more team efforts where shared sales credits are the only fair way to reflect the sales efforts of the many reps working together.

When IBM shifted to selling total solutions to customers, it had to alter compensation. IBM reps may sell not only computer hardware and specific application software, but help design an "integrated computer network" and then run it and maintain it for the customer after it is installed. Where IBM reps once were paid commissions based on an elaborate point system, encouraging mostly hardware sales, now they are paid on the basis of total "value-added sales, whether this is hardware, software, or services."[1] Clearly a change in IBM's market emphasis led directly to a compensation plan overhaul.

At Scott Paper, a different type of changed market emphasis required a brand-new reward system.[2] Reps in Scott's Consumer Products Division were once paid according to how all the accounts in a rep's assigned region performed. Scott recognized that its key retail chain accounts, most of whom operated across territory boundaries, required Scott reps who understood and could service their total needs as retailers. Scott wanted to become closer partners with these big accounts in order to assure itself of a continued solid share of the retailer's prized shelf space (for Scott brands). With this emphasis change, Scott began to reward its reps on the basis of how each key retailer sold Scott's products across all retailer locations and according to the merchandising and selling suggestions provided by the Scott key account reps.

In the cases of both IBM and Scott Paper, compensation and incentive plans had to be altered to recognize shifts in selling emphasis toward either full-line selling (IBM) or total customer-need coverage (Scott Paper).

Individualize Your Pay Plans

With compensation and incentive plans requiring continuous updating, and measurement systems becoming more complex with sales specialization, are there any general maxims sales managers should follow when designing their rep measurement-reward systems? In fact, there are some broad design principles that make sense for the volatile 1990s.

With high market instability (covered in earlier chapters) marked by wide differences in regional growth rates, industry business cycles, and distribution channel shifts, it makes sense not to put too much of any rep pay plan into a fixed pay plan such as salary. A blended approach that combines some salary (in recognition of those rep tasks without immediate or direct sales growth consequences) with some variable pay portion, probably provides the best compromise between short-term sales objectives and long-term goals for account development and sustained relationship building with customers. Straight commission plans make it difficult for reps to focus on anything but next month's sales quota. Long-term growth in new products or new account development almost always suffers because such activities have steep learning curves for reps. In addition, paying reps too much of their total pay as commission based on sales month to month requires that sales result measurements be absolutely above reproach in the company's accounting system. This is often unrealistic when the sales are to national distributors who are shared between several reps, especially when such distributors ship to their other branches from a central purchasing distribution center. The supplying company's sales are reported in accounting reports in one region, when in fact they may ultimately take place in several territories where the distributor operates. To alleviate measurement problems, sales are often pooled. But these systems can be very problematic when reps are paid 100 percent on commission. Arguments frequently ensue between reps about who gets credit for what portion of the distributor's total purchases.

Providing an excess (more than 65 or 70 percent) of a rep's pay in salary leaves a company vulnerable if either total market potentials for all reps or regional potentials between reps shift. The company will be caught with fixed expenses despite a variable situation—a surefire recipe for grief. In addition, "all reward, no risk plans," where salary is far too great a mix in compensation, make for high ongoing costs. For every dollar in salary, the company incurs another fifteen to twenty-five cents in benefit costs (pensions, life insurance, health care). Putting more pay into a variable part of the plan makes reps realize they must re-earn their money every year.

The watchword in pay plan design should be *flexibility*. By paying a rep a portion of his or her total income in salary, a manager retains the necessary control to guide reps in fulfilling all the sales basics required for total account service, including account retention. The "plus" portion of planned income that is variable can then be customized to specific performance goals. For some reps it can be fine-tuned to pay for finding new accounts, while with other reps it can be adjusted to pay for upgrading business with existing customers. The "extra compensation" can be paid differently depending on a rep's territory or sales tenure. So if the rep's growth prospects in a territory are poorer than those of other reps, the plus part of the compensation package can reflect lower growth expectations of the manager.

This plus portion of income can also be adjusted for any different product mix emphases desired by management in specific regions or with certain accounts. One company that manufactured and sold china dinnerware switched the incentive-pay portion of its reps' plans to encourage the sales of its full line. The company had determined that to continue paying simply on the basis of volume attainment was causing some reps to miss quotas on some lines, exceed on others, and still "max out" on extra compensation. This was creating chaos in factory scheduling and suboptimizing profits. The company opted to begin paying much higher extra compensation to reps whose combination of volume forecast attainment and product mix forecast attainment demonstrated sales of the full line. It did this by paying 70 percent of bonus compensation for going over forecast in total volume and another 30 percent for being among the top quarter of reps whose sales mix covered the broadest number of individual stock-keeping units. Those reps in the next quartile on "mix breadth" got less than the first quartile did, and those below these first two quartiles got no additional incentive dollars beyond their compensation based on volume. The company published rep rankings on the mix dimension, and within two years its sales force was selling a broader mix allowing more profitable and predictable plant volumes.

From a sales manager's perspective, the concept of blended plans is relatively simple to communicate to reps. The rep quickly learns that his or her base rewards day-in, day-out total selling functions, including duty at trade shows, keeping an eye on competitors, or making multiple calls over time to crack key accounts. The rep knows that the additional variable compensation is a customized, personalized issue that reflects his or her skills, workload, assigned region/accounts, and experience level. Such systems ring fair and comprehensible to reps. Should a company want to shift to a more variable pay scheme, it needs merely to boost the percentage of the total planned income that will be paid over and above the salary for sales target attainment. For instance, it could move from 30 percent extra compensation to 35 or 40 percent extra compensation beyond salary fairly easily in terms of altering plan calculations. If the company wishes to have the plan even more closely linked to *profit* results, it could pay compensation for performance based on total gross margins generated by the rep's results.

Another variation on such a scheme involves paying reps a portion of bonus compensation based on a mix of objectives up to some target *sales quota*. Once a rep moves beyond this quota, another piece of his or her income could be paid based on *gross margins* for volumes beyond the targets set. Paying extra compensation from incremental margins ensures that the scheme is self-liquidating. If sales managers do not wish reps to know gross margins, they can structure the payout based on the reps' ability to secure orders as closely as possible to "list prices." This encourages reps to sell without discounting prices and often accomplishes what payouts based on margins accomplishes, since premium prices are frequently a proxy for gross margin targets.

There are, of course, some variable commission schemes

that attempt to do the same thing, but are free of any salary-fixed cost commitments. And some companies would argue that this truly puts the onus on reps to make forecast in the products deemed most profitable, since commission rates can be adjusted by separate product line. The greatest drawback to such a scheme is that it fails to recognize that end-user customers often desire ongoing problem-solving assistance from reps (from which no direct sales will result). For instance, distributor accounts frequently want reps to perform a variety of key functions for them, such as training their staff on new products or applications that will help such accounts develop their territory and have longer-term sales impacts. But this offers no immediate sales commissions to the factory rep who did the training. In addition, reps on commission may resist training course enrollment that takes them off territories for any extended time. Any pay plan that diminishes the ability of a rep to develop with courses into more of a self-managed professional in the long run, is, counterproductive.

One expert has eloquently pointed out that a sales manager "should be proud to explain the sales compensation plan to customers."[3] This is frequently difficult to do for straight commission compensation plans, which often emphasize only part of the total selling job—new orders or customers. But all customers want to be perceived as more important to a rep than just the sum total of his/her last commission check. If commission structures are necessary to ensure plan affordability, the sales manager should try to see that commissions flow from both new orders or customers and existing *customer retention* (from the rep providing excellent after sales service). Otherwise the manager will agree with the objection of Casey Stengel, the great New York Yankee manager, to players who could play offense but not defense. Casey said, "I don't like fellas who drive in two runs and let in three."

The Complexity of Measuring Sales Results

If a company has a mix of selling approaches, the question of who should get sales credit for results is often complicated. For instance, if a sales force is specialized according to account size and territory, an account developed in a territory by one rep becomes another rep's account if it grows very large. If the selling company also has a telesales crew that handles supply orders for all customers, the large customer could have been developed by one rep, assigned to another, and its supply orders could be taken by still a third rep. How should sales results be measured for compensation purposes when quotas are being set and measured against actual volumes? It's already been pointed out that determining credit in sales territories can be difficult when national distributors take products from a supplier into a centralized warehouse and redistribute them to multiple locations. Several sales reps, from the supplying vendor and the distributor, may each deserve credit for some portion of the centralized orders brought into the distribution center. There are no hard-and-fast rules to follow to resolve this issue of measurement except to say:

1. Get a good controller/accountant on your side to try and help make assigned sales-credit calculations as unbiased and as reasonable as possible. Some calculations will never be perfect, but keep in mind that sales rep rewards are never wholly dependent on or tied to income rewards. Reps are also motivated by other incentives, such as advancement in the company, praise, meaningful two-way performance appraisals, and constructive coaching.

2. Choose sales measurements for compensation plan calculations that are available on a timely basis. Late sales reporting that holds up compensation checks will make for a frustrated sales force.

3. Select measurements that require as few complicated adjustments or calculations as possible. Reps should be able to quickly figure out their pay from "back of the envelope" arithmetic. If the rep needs software and a personal computer to calculate the performance-based portion of a pay plan, confusion and cynicism in the sales ranks will result. Reps have to be able to keep score by understanding how their sales results directly translate into their rewards. If

they don't understand the scoring system, they will not see the connection between their efforts, their results, and their compensation.

4. Sell the pay plan formula to the sales force. If it's got holes in it, they'll find them, and if it's fair, they'll react well to it. Plans that are somewhat imperfect in design but 100 percent accepted as fair and credible by reps are far superior to complex, "perfectly" engineered plans that nobody in the sales force really understands or accepts. A sales rep working for a major computer and office equipment maker received compensation pay quarterly based on a nine-page printout of services, parts, and equipment sold. When asked how he thought the plan worked in directing his sales effort, he replied, "I used to figure it out, but it wasn't worth the effort. . . . It gets so complex, I just shut down, pick up my briefcase and go sell."[4] This plan may suit the business, but it has certainly lost its performance improvement power.

Sales Incentives

More than two-thirds of American companies use cash and noncash incentives in addition to planned compensation to motivate sales reps.[5] They use short-term inducements for a variety of reasons. Special cash incentives usually are paid to push a specific product or land new accounts during a compressed time period. These incentives may be used to induce reps to shift product mix emphasis, to combat competition, overcome seasonal sales slumps, boost the sales of the most profitable lines, or ensure a new product gets a short-term boost in sales attention. Because new products usually take reps considerably more time to sell than do proven ones, short-term cash inducements provide the rep with positive reasons to take the time and win over customers to the new product. Cash incentives are becoming less popular however, because of their drawbacks. They are often less motivating than an expensive merchandise award, a trip prize, or a recognition symbol such as a ring, plaque, trophy, or desk set. The rep can show off merchandise awards or share the experience of a trip prize with others, if it was won by the entire sales team (including spouses). Reps remember the energy and work that went into the noncash recognition long after the cash award is spent (often to pay bills). If merchandise awards involve choosing from among a selection of prizes, the reps can put their own personal value on the prize, since it may represent something they would never buy even if they won a cash-equivalent award. They would simply be too practical and use the cash to reduce a debt, save for their children's college education, buy a new appliance, or purchase other useful, but not a "once-in-a-lifetime," item.

Trip prizes have "fantasy value" as motivators. They keep the rep thinking and identifying with the trip's benefits as he or she pursues extra sales performance. Where sustained performance, exceeding a few months, is desired by the sales manager, a trip prize motivates far more than do merchandise or cash awards. Trip prizes, combined with recognition awards publicly presented with fanfare to the outstanding achievers during the trip, are very motivating.

The Added Importance of Extra Recognition Rewards in the 1990s

Special recognition for extra sales achievements will be more important in the 1990s than ever before. There are many reasons for this. Downsizing is reducing opportunities to promote outstanding people—probably the most powerful and traditional way to provide recognition. In the 1990s, more than ever before, sales managers will need to recognize ambitious people by means of new challenges and enhanced incentive awards, in the face of reduced advancement opportunities.

Competition is tougher, and only companies with high sales productivity, low turnover, and the most motivated sales personnel will thrive. Salespeople become a competitive edge when product parity is widespread among competitors. In high-tech businesses, where short product life cycles prevail, the skills of sales reps often maintain a company's market standing when its products lose the technological edge. Rep skills really come into play in holding customer loyalties while company labs are producing a "next generation" product. One way to keep morale high is with special forms of recognition, a clear signal from managers of the standard of excellence they wish all employees to emulate.

Teamwork in selling is more critical, and because most pay plans recognize individual effort, teamwork excellence is best inspired by group incentives and recognition. Incentives can be flexibly structured to recognize nonrep members of the sales team, such as support personnel and dealer employees.

In an era of more rep and manager stress (covered in Chapter 6), special recognition often can be the tie that binds a rep to his or her company and generates a rarer commodity than gold–corporate loyalty.

Jack Falvey, a sales consultant, tells the story of a top-notch rep being wooed away from his current employer by another company that offered 30 percent more money. The rep turned the job down because he had set a personal goal for himself of earning a third diamond in his President's Club ring. He had earned two and had a space for a third. The recognition of earning the missing stone meant more to him than jumping jobs, even though the cost of an extra diamond was a miniscule part of the extra money he was being offered to change careers.[6] Recognition just makes good economic sense in an era of highly stressed reps, many of whom make excellent base levels of compensation. Recognition can have an incalculable value, because it can be earned only in special ways by an elite, chosen few. The essential difference between a pay plan and an incentive plan is that pay buys a rep's time and skills, while incentives buy enthusiasm and devotion, which are rarer commodities. Awards such as trips that involve spouses or families provide additional recognition. The role played by the family in supporting a rep during a peak sales drive (which usually involves considerable personal stress and work) can be handled nicely by including family members during trip awards.

Implementing Incentives

Given that incentive programs motivate and are taking on even more importance in an era of "lean and mean," the real issues revolve around how to design, schedule, and implement them to good effect. Here are some tips:

1. Determine early on how much of the recognition and incentive you want to go for team results as opposed to individual results. If your pay plans are already individualized, you may wish your incentive plans to recognize more of a team effort. For instance, the Boston Celtics basketball team does not pay its players individual incentives based on their personal scoring or other performance statistics (as many other teams do). The Celtics have never had the highest-scoring player in the league, but they've won more team championships than anyone else has. They have opted to recognize team effort instead of personal efforts. At a $17 million overnight express delivery company in Kearney, New Jersey, the sales manager lost the ability to get sales reps to work together and help each other as a team when the company got carried away with an overemphasis on *individual* bonus incentives. When a manager asked a rep to help a colleague, the attitude was "Forget it, I'm trying to make my bonus."[7] One sound alternative is to provide for individual recognition with status award programs (such as a "circle of excellence" for top sales reps, who can earn a plaque or ring) and a travel-trip incentive for team sales results, including all key team-support people.

2. Always opt for first-class awards/incentives and present them with "public" fanfare so everyone in the company is aware of them. If a quality effort is demanded to win an award, the design and selection of the prize should show the same high attention to "quality."

3. If a travel award is chosen, award winners should outnumber management or hosts on such trips; otherwise the travel award winners may question for whom the trip

was *really* arranged. Trip participation by nonreps should have a direct or obvious justification.

4. If a merchandise incentive plan is chosen, offer a cash alternative as a trade-in. It is too difficult to choose merchandise with universal appeal and utility for all the possible winners. Reps may already have color televisions, VCRs, microwaves, barbeques, or other usual prizes. And an unusual prize may not have any value or use to the winner. Reps close to retirement may not value a brand new sailboard. Nondrinking reps may place no value on an award of vintage wines. Because merchandise awards are often not as motivating as travel or status awards are, use them sparingly. Often overlooked awards that have universal appeal include investment instruments such as stocks and bonds.

5. Set goals for incentives that challenge participants but are within their reach. Any incentive program that doesn't fit this "fairness" test will fail. Lack of fairness is usually the single biggest complaint reps voice when discussing incentive plan design flaws. Never design a plan that favors top producers only.

6. Promote the incentive plan to ensure reps are totally familiar with the goals, rules, and ongoing results. A steady stream of reminders will bring optimum awareness and motivation. Send information on the program to reps' home residences, not through the internal company mail. In this way, the rep's family can be informed and involved, providing even more rep motivation.

7. Wherever possible, build "intermediate steps or awards" into any plan. This avoids an all-or-nothing scenario in which some outstanding intermediate performers never earn any recognition because final results fall off somewhat or the entire group misses the target.

8. Publicize ongoing results as the program progresses. This creates an atmosphere of steady, healthy competition. It also ensures that the program has chosen goals that can be measured and evaluated easily.

9. Always critique a program when it's over. Use a formal method of polling reps and hosts about the program

details, especially for travel awards where feedback about accommodations, services, the chosen location, and activities can help prevent any future problems sometimes encountered on such trips.

10. Always make sure that the budget for the program includes a portion of money to pay the tax owed by the winners on their award. There is nothing more demotivating than winning a big prize or a trip for outstanding sales performance, only to return home and face a big tax bill from the authorities. A motivator can turn into a demotivator very quickly.

11. Be careful about assuming that cash awards motivate *to the equivalent extent of other possible awards.* Perceptual problems accrue to selecting cash as a motivator, because many experienced managers believe it takes *more* cash than the identical cost of different awards to get the *same* results payoff.[8] Sales reps psychologically think of cash as income almost regardless of how the cash award is dressed up as recognition.

12. Never expect the incentive plan to do the whole job of the sales manager, directing efforts of reps. Motivating reps is always a combination of compensation and solid in-field coaching.

Incentives for Sales Managers

Not only sales reps benefit from incentive pay. Managers can also be powerfully motivated by them. Naturally, in the case of group incentives such as trips, managers who are supervising the winning team should be rewarded by their participation on the trip. But a great deal of thought is required in the area of individual incentive pay plans for sales managers, because sales managers can be so different in their task orientation. Some managers are routinely involved in hands-on selling to customers, and as such play a key role in bringing in key account orders. Other managers are much more involved in providing support to reps and in preparing sales plans and strategies, as opposed to executing these themselves or in tandem with their reps.

For managers whose involvement in selling actions is hands-on, incentives should be structured around the direct sales results of the reps and the manager. Typically a company should base incentive pay on a joint-results formula. The manager in effect earns incentive pay as a direct override on the sales commission or extra pay earned by his or her sales staff. This encourages the manager to provide hands-on training or selling involvement in line with direct results.

For a manager whose responsibilities in the field are more behind the scenes or encompass more of the management aspects of his or her title than do the sales aspects, bonuses should be based on a combination of goals attained. These could include attainment of sales targets for the quarter, gross margins for the quarter, and other objectives such as total new accounts opened as a percentage to target or new-product sales generated compared with expectations. The incentive pay becomes more of a management bonus program reflecting the stronger attention and time the manager spends on sales planning, new product launch planning, and product sales mix analysis and coaching.

Many companies do a poorer job structuring managers' pay than they do with frontline employees such as reps. In a national survey of middle managers (in multiple functions, not just sales), it was found that a great disparity existed between the desire of managers for "pay closely tied to their performance" and the actual existence of such plans at their place of work.[9] Over 89 percent said performance-based pay was very desirable, while only 55 percent said their companies structured their pay programs to reflect this desire.

With sales managers, the key to structuring such a plan is to have it reflect the task set they are expected to perform, be this "hands on" selling assistance or stronger "managing" involvement.

Sales Rep Performance Appraisals

Sales reps in the 1990s are becoming more professional, more service-oriented toward customers, and more self-managed. Many are specialists, better-trained and more targeted. As such they expect to be appraised on their performance in objective, professional, and constructive ways. And they expect to be active "partners" in this appraisal process—involved in rating themselves and providing their opinions on where they need to improve, alongside those of the manager. After all, salespeople are very much like professional contractors: They work for the customer. The reps take feedback from customers about what is satisfying their needs and then adapt sales solutions accordingly. The manager becomes less of an "authority" figure than the person working alongside the rep to help him or her develop and do the very best possible job to keep customers happy.

Many formal appraisals rate reps on a series of proficiencies, both quantitative and qualitative. These include skills in such areas as time management, paperwork handling, customer relations, expense control, holding onto customers and avoiding customer turnover, growing new accounts, and hitting sales forecasts.

These "laundry list" type appraisals fall down on two counts. First, they assume that reps with all of these well-rounded skills will succeed, which is not always the case in an age of narrower rep specialization. And second, they don't tie ratings specifically enough back to the manager's stated goals. Rep proficiency levels are only relevant if they are goal-directed. For instance, if a sales manager's goals are to grow sales to new accounts, the proficiencies necessary to produce this result among reps differ markedly from those necessary to hold onto and grow sales via "old-line" existing accounts. Each goal requires different kinds of training and daily call effort. Each would emphasize different field-level spending priorities in expense budgets. And each requires different skills in sales technique and paperwork handling. Figure 7-1 describes this concept in more detail.

To get maximum benefits from the appraisal process, managers need to be very specific about their goals and how these goals are to be measured. Managers who are very specific about their goals *before an appraisal* avoid surprising reps *during appraisals* about what their objectives are supposed to be. Second, identifying what measurement will be

Figure 7-1. Tying skill performance appraisals to key objectives.

Key Objective / Skill Emphasis	Grow New Accounts	Grow Business With Traditional Accounts
Training	How to spot and land new prospects; negotiation training (for handling price objections); training on selling your total company as a "quality" supplier.	Key account salesmanship; training in cross selling all products; training in team selling with other support functions such as customer or tech service.
Daily Call Effort	Must develop A, B, C classifications—Call emphasis is on intensive multiple calls/day, area by area, to define these priorities.	Cycle call frequencies and call productivity using existing customer lists and known buying potentials.
Expense Budget Emphasis	Spend on samples, sales aids, third-party testimonials from other new accounts; customer-"orientation" spending.	"Bundled" product proposals to upgrade accounts—spend to develop these; spend to provide customer with "value-added" services that lock in these long-time customers, such as electronic data interchange for order transactions.
Sales Techniques	Multiple calls, excellent at prospecting and securing product trials from new accounts.	Fewer calls, more in-depth, to boost sales per account and "upsell" product mix.
Paperwork Handling	Sales lead follow-up and reporting.	Understand/analyze detailed reports of product use per customer, buying frequencies by account, and changes in specifiers or influencers at each account.

used against these goals clarifies how performance will be determined against goals. Ratings won't be incongruous with performance because both rep and manager will have been looking at identical performance measures.

But measuring specific goals against actual performance ratings is just a start. Reps also need to know *how to improve*, from the manager's perspective. Do they need more training in a specific skill? Do they need to learn by immersion in some specialized assignment? Does the rep need to put out more effort in terms of calls per day or new account calls? Does the rep need more product training on new products in order to speed up sales of the new lines? Does the rep need to become more organized, more focused? Reps need feedback on how to improve *in as specific a form as it is possible to provide*. This is the only way for them to try to neutralize any negatives in their abilities, or to boost the application of any underutilized strengths they may possess.

One way to get reps more actively involved in the appraisal process is to ask them to do a self-appraisal prior to the appraisal meeting. This could include self-assessments of results, skills, and attributes, as well as training needs. The self-assessment can then form the basis of a two-way constructive dialogue between the manager and rep. If the rep's self-assessment is close to that done by the manager, the two are in lock-step agreement about rep development needs, shortfalls, and strengths. If the rep self-assessment is far apart from that of the manager, either the rep is quite out of touch with how he or she is performing or the manager and rep have developed a real communication problem about the manager's goals and ratings measurements. If, however, the gap cannot be explained by one of these two scenarios, than it can only have resulted from an unfair out-of-touch *appraiser*. The manager is then in deep trouble because he/she obviously doesn't know his or people (and is unfit to lead them). Figure 7-2 shows an example of a self-assessment form.

Peter Drucker maintains that the new manager must lead specialists just as an orchestra leader does, teaching people who all play to a different score how to harmonize. One of management's key challenges is to find such manag-

Figure 7-2. A rep self-assessment of performance (sample completed).

Date _____

Rep _____

Points   1–2   3   4   5
Rating   poor   fair   good   excellent

Results Section vs. Goals
(examples only)

Sales vs. forecasts	4
Growth in new products	5
Growth in new accounts	2
Complaint-handling resolution	5
Customer turnover	4
Expense control	4

Skills and Attributes Section

Selling skills	4
Product knowledge	5
Account knowledge	4
Industry knowledge	4
Competitor knowledge	5
Time territory management	3
Paperwork/records management	2
Relations with support staff	2
Creativity in resolving customer problems	3
Energy level/commitment to work ethics	5
Enthusiasm/assertiveness	4
Openness to new ideas	3
Decisiveness in selling situations	4
Maturity in judgments about customers	5

Training Needs Are?
Need courses in teamwork, more direction in managing account records and time-territory management.
Should work on tactfulness with other departments, perhaps a special assignment to let me get to know these people better and their key roles in supporting my efforts.

ers and to have them appraise in such a way that the specialist is involved in the appraisal, is clear about the goals for his or her specialty, and knows exactly how the orchestra leader believes he/she can improve individual performance to the assigned score.

Summary

A critical part of managing sales reps in the 1990s will be bringing out the best in the more professional self-managed specialist with pay plans, incentive programs, and performance appraisals. This chapter describes how to customize more variable pay plans (for reps and managers); how to make incentives work as rep and team inducements, to perform "above and beyond"; and how to set up a performance appraisal process that is a two-way active partnership between the rep and manager. When all three of these key management tools—pay, incentives, and performance feedback—work in tandem, reps are strongly motivated, goal directed, and receptive to the training and development so vital in today's harsher competitive selling climate.

Further Readings

Caballero, J. "A Comparative Study of Incentives on a Sales Force Contest." *Journal of Personal Selling and Sales Management* 8 (May 1988), pp. 55–58.

Johnson, Eugene, David Kurtz, and Eberhard Schering. *Sales Management.* New York: McGraw-Hill, 1986, pp. 394–415.

Kanter, Rosabeth Moss. "Rewards Reward Reward." *Boardroom Reports* (August 15, 1988), p. 8. The right way to reward employees using recognition.

Miller, Mary Lynn. "Increasing Marketing Productivity." *Conference Board Report* No. 86 (1981), p. 5. The productivity effects of altered procedures and rewards for sales reps.

O'Dell, Carla. "People Performance and Pay." *American Productivity Center* (1987) as reported in "Team Play—Team Pay—New Ways of Keeping Score" by Carla O'Dell in *Across the Board* (November 1989), pp. 38–45.

Quick, Thomas L. "The Best Kept Secret for Increasing Productivity." *Sales and Marketing Management* (July 1989). pp. 34–38.

Tubridy, Gary S. (of the Alexander Group, Inc.). "Management Briefing Marketing" (a bi-monthly briefing from the Conference Board), Vol. 4, No. 2 (April–May 1989), p. 5. Comments about basing reward systems on the twin dimensions of sales volume and gross margin percentages.

Verespej, Michael. "Executives Win, Workers Lose." *Industry Week* (July 17, 1989), pp. 19–26, especially page 23 on the impact of salary changes on benefit costs.

Chapter 8

Toward a World-Class Quality Sales Force

It's important that in the 1990s companies look beyond product quality and reliability. You not only have to have a better mousetrap, you have to have a better mousetrap manual, a better mousetrap delivery cycle, a better mousetrap training school, and a better mousetrap disposal service, and so on, if you want to be a leading successful company of the future.

—William L. Shippey
Executive Vice-President
Millipore Corporation Conference Board
BiMonthly Briefing
June/July 1989 (page 4)

The law of entropy holds that the universe tends naturally to disorder and chaos. Applied to the world of selling, it means that organizations are naturally in a process of falling out of touch with customers, markets, and trends because of the impermanence of life and events. Sales organizations, in order to battle the natural tendency to lose touch with customers and their needs, must make genuine and continuous efforts to understand customer expectations, and then meet and exceed these consistently. This is broadly defined as a "quality emphasis," the best antidote to the law of entropy. A quality emphasis introduces a formal structure to the process of knowing customers and using this information and knowledge to hold on to them.

"Quality" Management in Selling

Do you know what life would be like if people didn't strive for 100 percent quality? Even striving for 99.9 percent quality would mean that every hour the post office would lose 16,000 pieces of mail, O'Hare Airport in Chicago would have two unsafe landings per day, twenty-two thousand checks would be deducted every hour in banks from the wrong accounts, twenty thousand drug prescriptions would be wrongly prescribed every year, and fifty newborn babies would be dropped at birth by doctors each day. And that list doesn't include the thirty-two thousand missed heartbeats every person would experience per year.[1] While in North America a great deal of quality emphasis has been put into the process of making products, not nearly so much attention has been paid to emphasizing quality in selling products, except by service companies.[2] Certainly, on the logistics side of many companies, quality management has been instituted to improve order accuracy, to cut down on missed promise delivery dates, to cut order cycle times, and minimize incomplete shipments. All of these have aimed at closing the gap between customer expectations and actual corporate performance compared to these expectations. And the Japanese have taught the world that "doing it right the first time, all the time" also means designing the product from the customer's viewpoint, as the starting point. Rigorous attention to detailed customer feedback has led the Japanese to continuously improve their cameras, televisions, autos, copiers, machine tools, fax machines, steel, and integrated circuits.

But, in the world of selling, many North American companies have singularly neglected applying aggressive quality improvement programs in selling and sales management. In fact, many would struggle with defining what "quality selling" involves and how to achieve it.

Quality Selling Defined

A quality sales organization is one in which sales reps and managers have a deep knowledge of customer needs and use this knowledge to serve customers with care and understanding. The sales managers have welded together a team of salespeople and sales support staff who can consistently exceed customer expectations, so that quality buying experiences for customers and quality selling experiences for reps occur simultaneously.

While it is simple to state in concept, achieving such a quality selling state takes deliberate, consistent, and focused effort. A quality "buying" experience consists of three factors:

1. Customers believe that sales reps' *quality size-ups* of their needs and expectations are good.
2. Customers experience *fulfillment of these needs* on a right-the-first-time basis consistently over time due to the reps and the reps' support team.
3. When customer needs change suddenly, reps *respond to these contingencies in a quality way*, making every effort to meet the unforeseen contingency despite their inability to plan for it.

A "quality selling" experience occurs when:

• Reps believe their skills are the product of a first-class *quality training and development program*, so that they are equipped to size up and meet customer needs.

• Reps believe their skills and knowledge are a *good match for the selling challenges they have been assigned* by their manager. They are reinforced in this view by positive customer feedback.

• Reps believe they are respected as individuals and sales professionals with *"quality" in pay, recognition, delegation, and evaluation systems*. Quality, as reps would define it, involves fairness in rewards and recognition, honesty and two-way involvement in performance evaluations, variety in delegated sales assignments, and the manager's trust that the rep can handle such assignments well.

• Reps believe they are being led in ways that maximize "face-time" (that percentage of a rep's time spent actually face to face with customers) with customers and minimize wasted time or effort of any kind on their part. Reps sense that their managers really personally care about service to customers. L. L. Bean, founder of the sporting goods mail-order business that bears his name, used to consider customers part of his family. And he would personally charge around the company if a customer was dissatisfied with a purchase or service. There was no mistaking how this leader felt about quality—he wanted 100 percent customer satisfaction to be on all his employees' minds all the time.

Figure 8-1 models the concept of quality buying and selling experiences. The model is instructive. It shows that quality customer buying experiences depend on more than one component. Reps cannot only be good at understanding customers, or even at understanding them and fulfilling their usual needs—reps must also meet ongoing *unplanned* customer needs. Every customer contingency cannot be planned in advance, but how the contingency is handled can often determine the customer's perception of quality, in some cases for life. Larry Wilson tells the story of a sales rep in Japan[3] who sold a new Mazda to a customer only to learn that the customer's house had burned down that very night after the purchase. The rep went to the man's house, helped him salvage anything of value, and then was very understanding when the customer said he would have to cancel his auto purchase. A year later the customer returned to this same sales rep and bought another car, remembering the rep's help when the man's whole world had fallen apart. Since the initial sale, the customer purchased more than thirty cars and trucks for his company from the same sales rep. It is easy from such examples to understand why the Japanese word for customer, *okyakusama*, means "honored guest." The model suggests that it is quite possible to have a quality buying experience without a compensating selling

Figure 8-1. Quality buying and selling experiences.

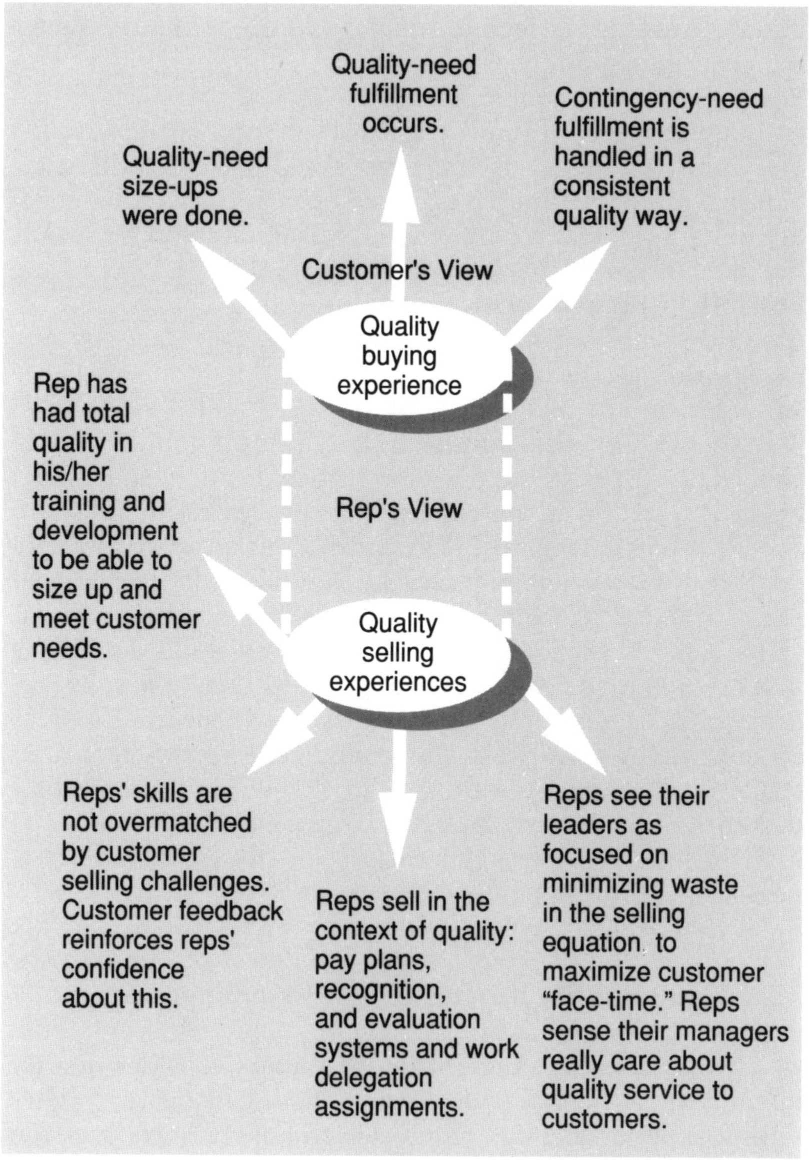

Quality-need
fulfillment
occurs.

Contingency-need
fulfillment is
handled in a
consistent
quality way.

Quality-need
size-ups
were done.

Customer's View

Quality
buying
experience

Rep has
had total
quality in
his/her
training and
development
to be able to
size up and
meet customer
needs.

Rep's View

Quality
selling
experiences

Reps' skills are
not overmatched
by customer
selling challenges.
Customer feedback
reinforces reps'
confidence
about this.

Reps sell in the
context of quality:
pay plans,
recognition,
and evaluation
systems and work
delegation
assignments.

Reps see their
leaders as
focused on
minimizing waste
in the selling
equation. to
maximize customer
"face-time." Reps
sense their managers
really care about
quality service to
customers.

experience, if the rep who is keeping the customer happy is not himself/herself happy. If the rep is stressed due to inadequate training, is feeling unfairly compensated or recognized or inadequately challenged, the selling experience may have been a hollow victory indeed.

Figure 8-1 also indicates, however, that a poor-quality "buying experience" is probably not possible at the same time a "quality selling experience" occurs. If customer needs are being routinely misdiagnosed, misunderstood, or simply not met, it would be difficult to imagine how a rep could possibly believe that his or her training, deployment, or direction were satisfactory. In addition, the rep's pay and recognition would certainly reflect customer disaffection, turnover, and below-sales forecast attainment.

The model also suggests that a total-quality selling experience for reps cannot be optimized unless sales managers are skillful at managing both processes and systems (e.g., pay plans, recognition systems, sales forecasting methods) as well as managing reps as individuals. The manager must be good at both interpersonal and communications skills as well as analytical and planning skills. Managing processes in a quality way is not of much use if the manager cannot manage people in a quality way. The reverse also applies: Being simply a sensitive and constructive recruiter, coach, and trainer is not enough if territories are poorly designed; accounts misassigned; sales forecasts lacking in realism; and rep pay plans lacking in equity, competitiveness, or motivating power.

Measuring Quality Buying and Selling Experiences

Given that one can define what customers consider quality buying experiences and what reps believe constitutes quality selling experiences, how can a sales manager know how the sales organization is doing to achieve total quality in both spheres?

There are a variety of methods to monitor each of these. The two best methods are to ask customers or reps for feedback on each dimension on a regular basis face to face when visiting or working with them, or to simply be watchful and observe those symptoms, which serve as "litmus tests" to indicate whether customers or reps believe themselves to be part of a quality experience.

Asking customers how you can improve the way you meet their needs usually provides valuable feedback, because the customers are usually not shy with ideas for improvements, many of which they may already be getting from your competition. When Motorola in 1986 asked customers how they liked dealing with the company, it got a great deal of feedback suggesting it was "hard to do business with." To improve, it gave all senior executives pagers so key corporate customers could reach them day or night. It authorized field repair crews to fix any defective Motorola two-way radios on the spot without home office approval if repair costs were below $1,000. And it altered its compensation plans for sales reps and managers to base some of their pay on buyer satisfaction figures collected in regular phone and mail surveys. Results show improvements in customer satisfaction ratings between 1986 and 1989. When Techsonic, the market leader in fish finders, asked its customers in focus groups, how to more successfully meet their needs, fishermen told them to make their products easier to control, easier to read in sunlight, easier to operate with gloves on in cold weather, and, on readouts, to clarify the displays so that fish could more easily be distinguished. Listening to customer needs helped grow Techsonic's sales from $11.5 million in 1983 to $70 million in 1988. Asking reps how you can help them deepen their knowledge of customers or of the sales organization's commitment to serving customers with care likewise gets reps talking positively about new and better forms of training, teamwork, specialization, call routing, account targeting, and inducements for customer retention, sales upgrades, and new "value-added services." If done systematically with formal surveys, benchmark measures of the current quality of selling can be determined and action plans put in place based on customer and rep ideas to improve these quality ratings.

For instance, one major manufacturer asked its end-user

customers and distributors to rate its sales reps' "quality"
on the following dimensions (relative to competitors):

- Their product knowledge
- Their industry knowledge
- Their product application knowledge
- Their ability to probe for customer needs
- Their ability to present products and make benefits
  apparent and relevant to each customer
- Their conduct, ethics, dress, and courtesy
- Their accessibility and availability to solve problems
  or answer emergency unplanned needs
- Their abilities to *resolve* problems that crop up,
  quickly
- Their responsiveness to customer complaints (such as
  product returns or credit problems)
- Their sense of confidence and pride of profession

The company discovered that while end users gave high
marks to reps, distributors gave much lower marks, because
reps were downplaying the need to do as high a quality sales
job with distributors as with end-consuming customers.
Reps were slow to return distributor phone calls, answer
complaints, sort out credit problems, or spend any time
training the distributors' reps about products. The company
took action to improve the reps' performance on these issues
and saw a marked improvement in both sales and the distributor's "quality buying experiences."

Simply observing how reps interact with customers, or
how they conduct themselves generally, can provide telltale
signs for how customers see reps and reps see themselves. A
sales force's pride, preparedness, and professionalism can
be evaluated as easily by observation as by any detailed
formal surveys or "rap" sessions with customers or reps.
Observation can reveal how well organized a rep is by view-
ing his or her car, briefcase, sample cases, and account
records. The rep's body language and eye contact with customers frequently reveal how confident the rep is with different products, how prepared to handle customer objections

he/she appears to be, and how good a listener and prober of customer needs he/she has become.

Another extremely useful way to gauge quality in buying or selling experiences is for sales managers to look for ratios that telegraph customer satisfaction or the state of rep skill development. These could include customer retention indexes, ratios of new accounts to old, the size of average sales per account (which can demonstrate rep proficiencies and may indicate enhanced customer responsiveness to selling efforts), items per order, add-on sales dollars, call to close ratios, volume of customer complaints, increases in "face selling time" percentages as a percent of total rep available time, volume of new-account cross referrals coming from existing customers, repeat-order volumes as a percent of total orders, amount of time before new reps become "selling" proficient, and so on. Some of these measures are surrogate indicators of quality training, coaching, or time management of the sales force. Others are direct measures of customer willingness to buy more products from reps, to actively refer new business to the company because of buying satisfaction, to buy from new reps in less time than it took in the past, to complain less, or to switch to the competition less willingly.

In measuring quality buying and selling experiences, it is crucial to use a mix of hard data and soft measures such as reps' morale, confidence in their product knowledge, comfort with new selling situations, and pride in their affiliation with the company. Soft measures of satisfaction include the way customers speak of your company and its products, their willingness to adopt your new products, and their eagerness to pass on ideas to your company about how to help serve them. Each measures how they view your company—whether they see you as open to "quality improvement" ideas, whether they will take it on faith that your new products will perform as advertised (in the absence of proof), and whether they are confirmed or skeptical users of your company's products.

Problems With Quantifiable Measurements

In tracking the quality emphasis of a sales force, there is often a tendency to rely too heavily on hard, measurable data and ignore less easily measured feedback about customer or rep satisfaction. It is all too easy to assume that hard number indexes that quantify the speed of customer service, number of complaints, or number of days training a rep receives are the best indicators of quality buying or selling experiences. But what if the customer's buying experience was enhanced mostly by the respect or kindness a rep showed to the buyer? What if the buying experience was enhanced because the rep worked to help the buyer sell his company on the rep's product and saved the buyer from doing something he may not have been very good at? Sometimes the less tangible, less demonstrable benefits brought to bear by reps on buyers are the ones the buyers value most.

Quality selling experiences work in the same way. An obsession by sales managers with measuring the quality of the sales force using only demonstrable, measurable indexes obscures the fact that reps are sometimes inspired to throw themselves body and soul into selling by a manager who demonstrates competitiveness, hard work, strong goal orientation, and a "hellbent for quality" attitude. The obsession Hallmark employees demonstrate today for quality is very much a derivative of founder Joyce Hall's own personal demonstrable obsession with quality products and customer service.[4] The impact of visible, committed sales leadership on a quality emphasis by sales reps should never be underestimated. Sales executives at IBM instruct their reps today that if any customer asks whether IBM can solve their computer hardware or software problem to *"just say yes."* IBM will then throw in whatever sales or technical resources are needed to make sure they deliver on this customer promise. This includes even recommending the use of non-IBM software or hardware as part of the system, if this is required to meet the customer's system needs.[5] Customers may not always be right, but sales reps should be encouraged to err on the side of customers. The motto of the Four Seasons Hotel chain, renowned for customer service, is "Nobody will ever criticize a staffer for making a guest happy."

Quality People Management

Sales management is a very hands-on type of profession, the ultimate "contact sport." As such, the manager often has a disproportionate impact on sales rep attitudes about what constitutes "quality selling." If sales managers want reps to be honest and ethical in all their customer dealings, their own behavior toward reps should set the example. If sales managers wish reps to be optimistic, calm, and pleasant in dealing with customers, they should demonstrate a friendly, pleasant approach with their own staff, not letting problems poison their outlook, being approachable and easy to talk to, and rarely becoming overexcited or flying off the handle. If sales managers want to teach reps teamwork, they should themselves be perceived as good team players, working smoothly with other departments and functions. If a manager criticizes the credit department or the accounting, manufacturing, or technical support functions, should he expect his reps not to mirror this attitude? Managers are role models for reps on ethical behavior, treatment and consideration of others' feelings, susceptibility to negativism, and even issues such as working hard. Managers who ask reps to make extra efforts and sales calls but who do not work overtime at their own jobs breed disrespect and alienation. Since all of these attitudes eventually rub off on customers, managers are wise to behave in ways consistent with those attitudes and behaviors customers value highly.

In some cases, teaching the right attitudes to reps does not go far enough in improving either the quality of an organization's selling or its customer's buying experiences. Recently Digital Equipment Corporation reorganized its customer contact teams into units aimed at serving specific target industries.[6] For instance, its regional manager in New York will supervise sales reps, systems engineers, and programmers who serve New York financial services companies. DEC has always encouraged team selling by all support people, but to provide an even better quality experience for customers, more than just attitudes were involved. It had to reorganize in order to tailor teams even more tightly to markets by region.

Thinking Quality: Emphasizing a "War on Waste"

Every production employee concerned about quality learns to deplore waste. Just-in-time manufacturing has eliminated

wasteful goods-in-process inventories. More statistical process control techniques have eliminated waste in raw material consumption during processing. Scrap, rework, and defect rates have been reduced with a variety of techniques,
from putting more onus on on-line operator quality control
than on postproduction inspection by others, to advanced
technology such as on-line vision systems that spot defects
early.

Sales managers and reps would do well to embrace this
mind-set of waging war on waste in all selling activities. One
study, for instance, showed that of one hundred customers
who had purchased products, 81 percent bought after the
fifth call and 10 percent after the fourth—so 91 percent took
at least four sales calls before the buyer placed an order.[7]
Clearly, any nonselling activities that take away from the
sales organization's core requirement to make persistent
calls is a potential form of waste. Conversely, any activity
that targets customers more efficiently or qualifies accounts
more precisely will enhance quality selling and buying experiences. Customers without real needs aren't bugged by
sales reps, and customers who have just bought and won't
be ready for repurchase for some time aren't called on, when
a "war on waste" mentality permeates a sales force. Sales
reps can wage war on waste by always making sure they are
calling on the right contacts in an account.

A "war on waste" mind-set also encourages reps and
managers to constantly ask themselves how to streamline
necessary paperwork that is not customer oriented and expense reports and meetings that can cut into total available
time for making sales calls. Managers need to fight to ensure
that reps can get time in the field. They need to stay in touch
with customer concerns and coach and train reps in real
selling situations. Although managers are often co-opted
into lots of meetings in the regional or head office, a "war on
waste" mentality can push them to question the importance
of attending such meetings, which take away from time-
consuming but often higher sales-leveraging duties such as
recruiting or field training.

Quality Sales Planning

Having a good, brief sales plan is one of the best ways for a sales manager to keep himself/herself focused on those strategies and tactics that boost competitiveness, improve quality in customer service, and promote "waste-free" selling.

A "quality" plan should comprise two parts. Part 1 is a synopsis of how the current sales organization measures up against competition and how it is performing compared to last year on important sales dimensions such as gaining new accounts, boosting sales per sales rep, selling more products per account, and sales by product/profit mix. Comparisons with competitors should include comparative size-ups of sales force strength, specialization, dealer/distributor network strength and relations, company reputation, teamwork at key accounts, and regional concentrations of sales coverage. These size-ups highlight where the company needs to improve in terms of physical account coverage, dealer/distributor contacts, and account strategy (specializing, team selling, and so on).

Part 2 of a "quality" sales plan involves briefly capsulizing the key strategies/tactics for each of the following sales-management challenges:

- Hiring needs by region/territory
- Training strategy
- Specialization emphasis/organization
- Target account plans
- Coaching needs of reps
- Product mix sales emphasis
- Dealer network improvements
- Special rep assignments/projects
- Compensation/incentive plan changes
- Recognition and contest programs
- Telesales issues
- Grooming reps for advancement/changes in reporting
- Sales and customer reports
- Automation of rep functions

The strategy would briefly describe action to be taken, whose responsibility such action is, what the timing will be, and how follow-up is to be done. An example strategy statement for rep hiring might state:

> Add a rep in N. East U.S., 2nd qtr. next year. Ask personnel to provide list of candidates for screening by self and 2 other sales managers. Follow-up 1st qtr. next yr.

Under training a strategy statement might state:

> Initiate refresher training on advanced selling skills for four reps who need it, by 3rd qtr. next year. Ask training dept. to coordinate arrangements. Follow-up *2nd* qtr. Stress coaching reps in how to sell higher ticket products to more senior executive customers. Do this with all reps by year end, and review with role plays at year end national sales meeting. Enroll self in course on financial skills for nonfinancial managers by 2nd qtr. next yr.

Such tightly crafted plans are excellent tools to help a sales manager remain focused and committed to improved quality by better planned efforts and priorities.

Summary

Quality is being pursued vigorously by businesses as a lever against competition. Doing the right things right the first time is the key to retaining and gaining customers. While much has been done with quality programs in the factory, attention to them in field sales forces has been minimal among manufacturers. This chapter defines what constitutes a quality selling operation, how this can be measured using both hard data and softer measurements, and how critical the role of a sales manager is in emphasizing both quality people management and a quality mind-set among reps. Managers can apply to field selling activities the same type of aggressive war on waste that the factory uses. In addition, by doing some quality planning, the sales manager can zero in on the focused priorities that need attention if customer expectations are to be consistently surpassed.

Further Readings

Crosby, Philip B. *Quality is Free*. New York: The New American Library, Mentor Books, 1979.

Department of Trade and Commerce, U.K., under auspices of Cecil Parkinson, Secretary of State for Trade and Industry, *The Case For Quality*. London: Alpine Press, 1983. This tightly crafted article capsulizes the sum of quality, function by function. The key role of the field sales force in knowing customer needs and feeding back continuously on meeting these needs is also discussed.

Hyatt, Josh. "Ask and You Shall Receive." *Inc.* Magazine (September 1989), p. 90.

Juran, J. M. *Managerial Breakthrough*. New York: McGraw-Hill, 1964.

Murphy, John R. "Management Education as a Strategic Weapon." *Training* (February 1989), pp. 47–54. Covers GTE's quality improvement plan and the required culture change necessary to implement it.

Schein, L., and M. Berman, eds. *Total Quality Performance. Conference Board Report* No. 909, 1988.

Sellers, Patricia. "Getting Customers To Love You." *Fortune* (March 13, 1989), pp. 38–49. Profiles quality improvements by customer satisfaction oriented companies including H. B. Fuller, Techsonic, Land's End, Four Seasons Hotels, Northwestern Mutual Life, Domino's Pizza, Saab-Scania of America, DuPont, Motorola. For an in-depth review of how Techsonic used focus groups of customers to improve their business, see Hyatt, Josh.

Postscript

The Changing
Sales Manager's Job

The last half of this book has dealt with the many ways in which sales managers must alter their skills, priorities, and practices to cope with a new generation of sales reps and a more demanding, competitive business climate.

It is useful to summarize these changes and contrast sales management for the 1990s with sales management in earlier years. This is most easily explained using Figure P-2, where the key preoccupations and challenges of sales managers are displayed from the past to present and future realities.

Figure P-2. Sales management priorities and practices over time.

The Way It Was	*Today and in the Future*
Recruitment and Selection	
• Hire strong individualistic reps for territory placement. • Look for generalist education, with an aptitude for selling. • Hire mostly men. • Hire high school graduates with some selective college courses.	• Hire team-oriented personnel. • Hire specialists including telephone sales reps and key account executives. • Hire a mix of women and men. • Hire people with college degrees as a prerequisite, in many cases.

The Way It Was	*Today and in the Future*

Training

- Few key courses in sales techniques, time management, and product knowledge provided to reps.
- Training in short duration courses; "refresher" training only provided periodically.
- Classroom-type training settings predominated.

- Wide array of new courses including "systems sales," "dealing with distribution," "how to size up competitiors," studying target industries of reps' assigned customers, etc.
- Back-to-school-type training is continuous.
- Training is in multiple modes including self-study, interactive video, and other emerging techniques.

Goal Setting and Planning

- Sales goals set by territory and individual reps, based upon similar selling methods and independence between reps.

- Sales goals set differently by type of selling: telesales, national account selling, system selling, or specialized selling by distribution channel.
- Team sales goals are set in addition to sales assigned individually by rep.

Sales Rep Deployment and Direction

- Territory potentials were calculated yearly, updated only rarely, and territory potentials were often not optimally balanced between reps. Reps were directed via in-person visits, sales meetings, and via telephone.

- Computers are used extensively to analyze account and territory potentials, and then to match up manpower assignments. Reps are often deployed so that they have both territory responsibility for many accounts and cross-territory responsibility for regional or large accounts.

(continued)

Figure P-2. continued.

The Way It Was	Today and in the Future
	• Rep direction often is provided by electronic mail or using other means such as laptop computer linkages. In-person visits with reps are shorter and more intense as the sales manager has more people reporting to him or her (due to "lean 'n' mean").

Coaching Reps

The Way It Was	Today and in the Future
• Coaching was often done via a "watch-me sell" approach. Managers were often heavy handed with reps: They had a command-control mentality. Managers coach the reps on "how to" close, "how to prequalify accounts," "how to probe for customer needs," etc. All these coaching tips were "how to" specific.	• Less autocratic, more empathetic; reps are treated as "territory managers" or "account managers," and the sales manager listens and accepts the reps' inputs about how to satisfy these accounts. Managers must be more tuned in to the individual rep's higher level of personal stress (due to two-career couples and more competitors). Managers coach reps on learning how to "learn" versus how to "perform" specific sales tasks.

Measurement of Rep Performance

The Way It Was	Today and in the Future
• Performance appraisals were one-way: manager to rep. Measurements were simple (sales vs. quota) and individualized.	• Team measurements become more common. Measurements are broader than just sales results such as "customer satisfaction" measurements. Performance appraisals are more two-way and participatory in nature,

The Way It Was	*Today and in the Future*
	with reps taking on more responsibility for defining their own strengths, weaknesses, and needs.

Pay

• Variable portion of pay plans were often 10, 15, or 20 percent of total rep pay package.	• More variable pay plans with a smaller fixed salary as a percentage of total pay plans. Today, often more than 30 to 40 percent of income is dependent directly on attaining specific sales objectives.

Sales Rep Recognition

• Sales managers used mostly prizes and cash awards to induce extra efforts. These prizes were structured for the dominant method of sale: the territory rep.	• Sales managers use incentive trips and stress the involvement of entire divisional teams in recognition programs. Families are often included in sharing such incentive trips.

Sales Rep Promotions Into Management

• A rep remained as a career salesperson or was promoted into a district or national sales force management position.	• Reps are promoted into any number of sales specialties (including trainer positions). • A dual promotion ladder is created, so that reps can progress in status and pay without having to aspire to management jobs.

As can be seen in Figure P-2, virtually every major sales management area has been changed. Sales leaders with adaptability and courage are transforming themselves from front-line command and control managers to "network" managers who coordinate varied teams of self-managed sales professionals. In this world, "span of communication" becomes more critical than "span of control." And learning to manage a more diverse group of reps in tighter, more complex customer relationships separates the truly great sales managers from the also-rans.

Notes

Chapter 1

1. Louis Rukeyser, "Time Traveller in U.S. Today Wouldn't Know Many Firms," *Toronto Star* (September 10, 1988), p. C3.
2. John Case, "The Disciples of David Birch," *Inc.* magazine (January 1989), p. 45.
3. Myron Magnet, "The Resurrection of the Rust Belt," *Fortune* (August 15, 1988), quoted from Governor Richard Celeste of Ohio, p. 40.
4. John Case, p. 44.
5. Dyan Machan, "How Gus Blythe Smelled Opportunity," *Forbes* (October 3, 1988), p. 113.
6. John Hoerr, "Work Teams Can Rev Up Paper-Pushers, Too," *Business Week* (November 28, 1988), p. 28.
7. N. Tolson (of Du Pont), "Good Sales Team Knows Customers Inside Out," *Marketing News* (November 21, 1988), pp. 5, 11.
8. Christopher W. L. Hart, "The Power of Unconditional Service Guarantees," *Harvard Business Review* (July–August 1988), pp. 54–55.
9. Miland M. Lele, *The Customer Is Key* (New York: John Wiley & Sons, 1987), p. 72.
10. Tom Richman, "Seducing the Customer—Dale Ballard's Perfect Selling Machine," *Inc.* Magazine (April 1988), p. 102.

Chapter 2

1. "Cheap Asian Imports Flood Japan," *Wall Street Journal* (July 20, 1988), pp. 1, 17.

2. "Market for Large Sized Women's Clothes Tops 10 Billion," *U.S.A. Today* (July 29, 1988), pp. 1B, 2B.
3. "Ford-Nissan Plant for Mini-Vans Expected to Be Built in Cleveland," *Toronto Star* (September 10, 1988), p. C3.
4. Kate Bertrand, "Sony: Sorting Out the Sales Suspects," *Business Marketing* (August 1988), p. 46.
5. "Average Cost of Sales Call is Two Times U.S. in Western Europe," *International Management Journal* (May 1988), p. 15.
6. Earl Bailey, "A Growing Role for Business-to-Business Telemarketing," *Conference Board* Report No. 912 (1988).
7. "Telemarketing is 'Smarter' When Used With Other Tools," *Marketing News* (August 15, 1988), p. 8.
8. G. Whatley, "Hot Telesales Force," *Chief Executive (U.K.)* (February 1988), pp. 28–32.
9. Steve Zurier, "Dialing for Dollars at J. Fegely," *Industrial Distribution* (May 1988), pp. 105–107.
10. Marina Strauss, "Pillsbury Canada Makes a Fresh Start," *Globe and Mail, Report on Business* (December 5, 1988), p. B1.
11. Lea Strazewski, "Apple Uses New Marketing Strategy to Take a Slice of Competition's Pie," *Marketing News* (September 12, 1988), pp. 7–8.
12. Linda Cardillo Platzer, "Managing National Accounts," *Conference Board Report* No. 850 (1984), p. 19.
13. Al Urbanski, "America's Best Sales Forces," *Sales and Marketing Management* (June 1988), pp. 42–43.

Chapter 3

1. Steve Zurier, "Selling All the Buying Influences," *Industrial Distribution* (August 1988), p. 37.
2. Ibid.
3. J. Bonnanzio, "The High Tech Market," *Industrial Distribution* (September 1988), pp. 30–43.
4. "Toyota Wants to Teach Dealers to Sell One Used Car for Every New Car Sold," *Automotive News* (July 1988), p. 48.
5. "Supermarket Listing Criteria" (a report by Touche Ross and Company), *Advertising Age* (August 1988), p. 12. (For a more complete outline of retailer listing criteria.)

Chapter 4

1. Jag Seth and S. Ram, *Bringing Innovation to Market* (New York: John Wiley & Sons, 1987), pp. 17–18. (For a fuller discussion of technological ages.)

2. Christopher Knowlton, "Consumers: A Tougher Sell," *Fortune* (September 26, 1988), p. 74. The other five markets were high-definition TV, home satellite dishes, generic drugs, fat substitutes, and outpatient storefront clinics.
3. Thayer C. Taylor, sr. ed., "Computers in Sales and Marketing," *Sales and Marketing Management* (May 1987), p. 5.
4. "The Market for Video Conferencing," *New York Times*, (November 10, 1985), pp. F6, F7.

Chapter 5

1. "Women Keep Coming On," *Sales and Marketing Management* (February 1989), p. 26.
2. "Women Keep Coming On," p. 26.
3. Steve Fishman, "The Longest Sale," *Success* magazine (May 1989), p. 50.
4. Ibid., p. 50.
5. Fred J. Jespersen, "A Sales Manager Sets His Sights on Bigger Game," *Business Month* (June 1989), p. 96.
6. S. Shipp, K. Roering, and R. Cardozo, "Implementing a New Selling Mix," *The Journal of Business and Industrial Marketing*, 3, 2 (Summer 1988), pp. 55–63.
7. Richard Kern, "The 1990 Census: The Good, The Bad, and the Undercount," *Sales and Marketing Management* (July 1989), pp. 49, 50.
8. P. Sinha, and A. Zoltners, "Matching Manpower and Markets," *Business Marketing* (September 1988), pp. 95–98.
9. Susan Benway, ed., "Small Business Has Merger Mania Too," *Business Week* (May 13, 1989), p. 61.
10. David Perry, "How You'll Manage Your 1990's Distribution Portfolio," *Business Marketing* (June 1989), pp. 52–56. (For a good description of this phenomenon.)

Chapter 6

1. Mac Anderson (ed.), *The All-Time Greatest Sports Quotes, Volume One* (Lombard, Ill: Great Quotations, Inc., 1984), p. 529.
2. Charles Ames and James D. Hlavacek, *Market Driven Management* (Homewood, Ill.: Dow-Jones Irwin, 1989), as excerpted and adapted in *Success* magazine (May 1989), p. 20.

3. H. Sujan, B. Weitz, and M. Juran, "Increasing Sales Productivity by Getting People to Work Smarter," *The Journal of Personal Selling and Sales Management* (August 1988), p. 11.
4. Stanley J. Modic, "Motivating Without Promotions," *Industry Week* (June 19, 1989), p. 27.
5. Arthur Lipper III, "Leaders—A Riper Apple," *Venture* (May 1989), p. 5. An interview with John Sculley, CEO of Apple Computer Inc.
6. Thomas L. Brown, "In Search of Failure," *Industry Week* (January 16, 1989), p. 26.

Chapter 7

1. John W. Verity, "A Bold Move in Mainframes," *Business Week* (May 29, 1989), p. 77.
2. "America's Best Sales Forces," *Sales and Marketing Management* (June 1989), p. 43. (For a profile of Scott Paper's Consumer Products Division Sales organization.)
3. Thomas R. Mott, quoted in *Sales and Marketing Management* (February 1989), p. 63.
4. Jerry McAdams, "Rewarding Sales and Marketing Performance," *Management Review* (April 1987), p. 35.
5. Ibid., p. 34. (From national survey of 1,600 U.S. companies in industries representing more than 20 percent of total GNP.)
6. Jack Falvey, "It's Loyalty That Binds the Sales Force Together," *Sales and Marketing Management* (July 1989), pp. 24–25.
7. Joshua Hyatt, "Growing Up as a C.E.O.," *Inc.* Magazine (July 1989), pp. 60–70.
8. Jerry McAdams, p. 36.
9. Leslie Brokaw and Teri Lammers, "What Motivates Managers?" *Inc.* Magazine, (June 1989), p. 115. (A survey by the American Productivity and Management Center.)

Chapter 8

1. Jeff Dewar, of QCI International, has come up with these examples; see Bruce G. Posner, "Why 99.9% Just Won't Do," *Inc.* Magazine (April 1989), p. 26.
2. See, for example, *The Conference Board Research Report* No.

909, 1988, "Total Quality Performance," edited by Lawrence Schein and Melissa Berman. Customer-driven quality discussions involve almost no mention of the selling process nor of sales management.

3. Larry Wilson, *Changing the Game: The New Way to Sell* (New York: Simon & Schuster, 1989), in section on "adding value."

4. Keith D. Denton, and Barry L. Wisdom, "Shared Vision," *Business Horizons* (July–August 1989), p. 68.

5. Joel Dreyfus, "Reinventing IBM," *Fortune* (August 14, 1989), p. 35.

6. Leslie Helm, "DEC Has One Little Word for 30,000 Employees: Sell," *Business Week*, August 14, 1989, p. 86.

7. "Sales Talk," *Sales and Marketing Management* (July 1989), p. 82.

Index

A. B. Dick, 35
account management, national,
43–51, 109, 127
accounts, tracking changes in,
127–128
A. C. Nielsen, 62
acquisitions, 128
adaptive selling skills, 142
Advanced Marketing Services
Inc., 72
aggressive competitors, 141
Air Products Corp., 113–114
Allegheny Beverage, 87
American Airlines, 84
Sabre reservation system, 85
training by, 123
American Express, 5, 64
Apple Computer, Inc., 8, 38–39,
116, 144
appliance industry, 6
appointment selling, cellular
phones and, 81–82
Armstrong World Industries, 89
Arrow Electronics, 58
Atlanta, Georgia, 11
Austin, Texas, 11
auto industry, 13
Automatic Data Processing
Inc., 51
awards
for achievement, 110
cash, 156–157, 161

for groups, 158
of merchandise, 157, 160
quality and, 171
recognition, 34, 157–158
for sales managers, 161–162
system of, 149–167
tax bill on, 161

Ballard Medical Products, 22–
23
banking deregulation, 12
Bearings Inc., 58
Beaver, Donald, 9
Becton Dickinson, 43–44
Bell & Howell, 36
Bell Atlantic Corp., 121
solutions selling by, 16–17
Bennis, Warren, on goals, 144
B. F. Goodrich Co., 4
biotechnology, 9
Birch, David, on job creation, 8
Black and Decker Corp., 14
Boeing Co., 21
bonds, as awards, 160
Boston, Massachusetts, 11
Boston Celtics, 159
Briggs-Weaver Co., 68
Brock, William, *The Economics
of Small Business*, 8
building contractors, 80
Burlington Industries Inc., 6–7
training by, 123